Get A
Better Job!

Get A Better Job!

by

Arthur Wilcox and John Clarke

Contents

Part 1

*We begin with school-leavers, but if you've left school
far behind don't let that deter you.
You may pick up some useful tips.*

Part 2

Here we deal with more sophisticated job-hunting.

Part 3

*Here we deal with the most important element of all,
the CV (or Résumé).*

Introduction

This book will help all who seek a job, whether a first job, a better job or merely a different one. It is of special use to those who are unemployed, and will also benefit those seeking a place on a Government-sponsored training (or re-training) scheme. The ideas which the book gives will assist the interview technique of those seeking entry to university.

Before starting on the subject in hand, a word about sex discrimination: in writing a book of this nature it would be extremely cumbersome to have to say 'he or she'/'him or her' at every point throughout the book. Therefore I have opted for the simpler and general 'he'. This does not mean that the information is not relevant to both sexes, and no bias is intended; it has been done simply for ease on the reader's eye!

Job-hunting has a high built-in failure rate. When six candidates are interviewed for one job, five must be rejects. Yet these five are among the best in the field.

How can an applicant prevent the long odds against him from sapping his confidence? Answers to this question are particularly important for the school-leaver who has worked his way up the school and achieved a position of some responsibility and perhaps some authority, and whose first experience of trying to enter the confusing and competitive world of work marks him down as a 'failure'.

They are no less vital for the person who has lost his job and may face a long period on the unemployment register unless he goes into action quickly and effectively.

He might shorten the odds by putting in for as many jobs as he can. If he adopts this hit-or-miss practice, he will get a job in the end, but his disappointment may start when he realizes that it is the wrong job.

The best thing he can do is to study the market for jobs in his particular line and in his own locality (or further afield, if he is prepared to move), to select his targets realistically, and to prepare his written application and his performance at interview with the utmost care.

The more efficiently he presents himself – on paper and in personal contact – the better will be his showing in the labour market. He can rest assured that an employer is just as anxious to pick the right worker as he is to pick the right job.

Interviewers of all levels and ages of applicant sometimes find that they have regretfully to turn down candidates with a great deal to commend them. Their reasons for rejecting a candidate might begin:

'I liked him, but . . .'

'Why didn't anyone advise him . . .'

'Didn't he realize that . . .'

'What a pity he hasn't got (some qualification or ancillary subject, certain experience, or some personal quality vital for the job)'.

They might end by saying 'He'll make a good career somewhere, but not with us'.

Often, these things can't be helped. At interview it's too late. You can't produce a missing qualification especially for interview, nor gain precious experience, but you can at least prepare yourself and show yourself to best advantage.

The worst case of all, because it could so easily have been remedied, is that of the person who possesses all the basic qualifications, experience and know-how, and enough of the personal qualities to make him a fair prospect, but who somehow doesn't present himself well at interview.

8

This might not matter in a poor field, but it does matter when it is a toss-up between two or more candidates. It could so easily turn out that the worse is picked and the better rejected, simply because the former comes over more positively. The fact that he comes over positively is, of course, in his favour, but performance at interview does not represent faithfully the qualities needed in the job itself.

To be sure, the rejected candidate, like the selected one, knew in advance that the interview was a crucial situation. Crucial or not, for many people it is rather an unknown situation, hedged with speculation, rumour, gossip, fears, and something of a mythology. What the interviewer thinks, what he is like, what he really wants, what the interplay between interviewer and interviewee is going to be like and the course it will take – all these are unknown. All the same, a candidate can prepare himself, and think out likely eventualities in advance. Careful preparation may spare a candidate regrets later on.

Unemployment

Unemployment is a major problem throughout the Western World. Any recovery in economic activity may well *not* produce a corresponding increase in employment opportunities because of the impact of high technology. Fewer workers will be needed, but they will be more efficient and more flexible.

This is bringing a change in career patterns. There is more retraining. 'A job for life' is becoming a thing of the past. Career structures within companies are altering and internal development schemes are increasingly taking the place of 'paper' qualifications (provided the minimum standards are achieved).

It is likely that opportunities in the future will go to those who can learn new skills and adapt to the changed requirements of the labour market.

Examinations of an applicant's 'track record' combined with an interview assessment remain the traditional way of choosing. Thus the applicant must prepare a plan to display his or her experience – and potential – to best advantage.

This book, therefore, contains useful advice for candidates for interview at whatever level; from the raw school-leaver looking for his first job or sparring for selection to a job experience scheme, to the professional person looking for a better one. Wherever you come in this spectrum, it should give you some of the know-how and confidence you need.

It starts, where we all start, with the school-leaver.

Part 1

We begin with school-leavers, but if you've left school
far behind don't let that deter you.
You may pick up some useful tips.

1

Finding That Job

STAGE ONE: SEEKING INFORMATION

While you are still at school

School library
 (i) Careers books and pamphlets.
 (ii) Booklets setting out career prospects with local firms and industries.
 (iii) Books of a general nature which throw some light on careers.

School staff
 (i) Teachers of particular subjects will know about employment prospects of young people who have followed courses in those subjects and have perhaps gained qualifications in them.
 (ii) There may be a careers teacher on the staff of your school. He may be full-time or, more likely, part-time. If there is no careers teacher, the Head, Deputy Head, or perhaps a Housemaster may give careers advice. If there is no teacher who you feel can help you, and no notice referring to careers on the notice board, try the school office. Quite often a school establishes a useful connection with local firms. A firm may inquire whether the school can

recommend a promising boy or girl in their particular line of business. Or it can work the other way round: a Head who knows that boys or girls in the past have done well with particular firms, may recommend likely leavers to these firms. Either way round, the school office is a 'clearing house' for information and perhaps actual applications.

Services offered by or through the school
(i) Visiting speakers who talk about employment prospects in commerce, industry, and the various services. Their help is not limited to a lecture. They answer questions, leave pamphlets or other hand-outs for reading at leisure, and organize personal contact where this is called for.

(ii) Visits by groups of young people to various places of work. These are specially important because they can see for themselves and ask questions on the spot. Such visits are often brief, but they are sometimes extended to provide valuable work experience in an authentic setting.

(iii) Leavers' conferences (under this or some other name) by which leavers (and their parents, if the meetings are held in the evening) hear about job or Further Education prospects in the locality. These are useful occasions for meeting representatives of firms and other bodies to discuss practical matters.

(iv) Meetings with Careers Officers and school staff connected with employment.

Looking after your personal interest
(i) Find out what jobs are possible with your interests, the courses you have followed at school, and exam and other achievements.

(ii) Find out what jobs you are interested in, but are ruled out for you because you haven't the right qualifications. Can you make up any missing qualifications if you are really keen on one of these jobs?

14

(iii) Discuss with anyone able and willing to help you the pros and cons of the various jobs you are interested in. Don't let anyone make up your mind for you. All the same, take advice seriously, from whatever quarter it comes. From all the possibilities, you must narrow the choice to one! (You will find in practice that there are all sorts of limitations on your choices: e.g. the employment situation in your locality.) Don't forget to contact a few of those who are a year or two older than you are, and are already at work, so you can be guided by the practical experience of people who were once in your position. They will be able to tell you of unexpected snags that turned up, as well as things that went unexpectedly well.

While you are still at school/when you have left school

Local library
 (i) Careers books.
 (ii) Use the library's information service. The library offers a wider service than you might suspect. Where they cannot provide the sort of detailed information you might want, they are able to put you in touch with organizations, firms, etc., who can.
(iii) The library will almost certainly have a wider range of local newspapers than you take at home. Look through the advertisements offering jobs.
(iv) Study local directories and the 'yellow pages' of the telephone directory to see what firms there are of the sort you want.
 (v) See if there are local Schools/Industry liaison groups providing contact between Head Teachers and senior industrialists. Some of these provide additional resource centres in libraries and schools.

STAGE TWO: ACTING ON YOUR INFORMATION

(i) Learning about likely jobs from advertisements, the Careers Service, personal contact, etc., and telephoning for an interview or sending in an application.

(ii) Telephoning, writing, or calling at the premises of a likely firm (or office, etc.) even though no job is at present being advertised. You will get an idea of when one may turn up for a person of your age and qualifications. You may get a useful insight into the way young people are taken on, by talking to the personnel officer (or training officer, or education officer, etc.) of a large concern.

(iii) When a job is really on the cards, mount your own personal 'campaign' for achieving it, using the advice given in this book. Your campaign will be, at its simplest, a telephone call arranging for an appointment, your own self-preparation, and the interview. At a higher level, it will include sending for an application form (or writing your own application if there is no form), getting your testimonials and exam certificates ready, arranging for referees, preparing yourself for interviews and making a success of it when it comes.

(iv) Don't be afraid to have out two or more applications at the same time. You must look after your own interests here, and you can't afford to let time slip by while a firm is considering an application from you.

(v) In consultation with the Careers Office, you may be able to obtain work experience with a particular employer whose work suits you, and this could lead to permanent employment later.

How Far Can Parents Help?

Many schools hold careers conventions (or conferences) at which parents and young people together can learn, from the people concerned, about prospects in local industry and commerce, and in various other occupations. Such meetings are exploratory, and questions can be asked and interest shown without the young people committing themselves in any way.

Parents are a real help here, because they can often ask more knowledgeable questions than their children can, and follow them up on their children's behalf. At a careers convention it is the representatives of firms, etc., who are on show rather than the young people themselves. They are as anxious to put their kind of work in a good light as candidates are to show themselves attractively. If it comes to it, the school leaver (or his parents) can put them through the same kind of grilling as he himself may fear, drawing out the details of just what they want to know.

It might seem as though the role of parents could be the same in an interview situation as it is at a careers convention. After all, the parents could chip in at an interview, adding support to their son's (or daughter's) case, prompting him with points he might be too forgetful or too timid to put on his own behalf. However, most employers would not expect to see the parents at an interview. It is the young person as an individual they are wanting to employ – not as a team with parents in tow.

A first interview (like first love) can seem a traumatic experience at the time. (If it does not appear like this, it might be because the candidate takes it too lightly, or doesn't realize its importance; in most cases, though, the shock is softened by preparation on the part of the candidate.) In an advisory interview, or any meeting that does not commit you, parental support may well be a help, but for the interview where you commit yourself the most sensible advice is: Go it alone.

2

Writing About That Job

First impressions count, and the first impression that your future employer gains of you comes from your letter applying for the job or asking for an appointment. How do you want to appear to him? It is worth taking trouble to present this preview of yourself as attractively as possible.

Much of what you are going to say will be contained in your CV, and this subject is so important that I devote the whole of Part 3 of the book, starting on page 133, to it.

In Part 2 I shall explain how to apply for a job where we are dealing with candidates seeking professional posts or trying to improve their job by moving to another one.

Who Are You?
Obviously the person who has been at work for some time has got more of a track record and his CV could be quite a comprehensive and detailed document.

For the school-leaver the track record is more difficult since you have not got much experience yet, but everybody has some sort of experience that is useful information for a prospective employer.

Make up a CV including in it all the matters of general interest which could be useful information to any prospective employer. Then, when you apply for a job, all you need to do is to write a short letter to accompany the CV.

Draw up your CV with care, type it out (get a friend or relative to if you can't), and get plenty of copies.

The CV should contain the following:—

1. **Name, Address and Telephone Number (if any).**
2. **Date of Birth.**
3. **Schools attended.**
4. **Examination results, especially GCSEs.**
5. **Details of any part-time or Saturday jobs which you have done.**
6. **Details of any hobbies or interests, especially if these might be useful adjuncts to employment.**
7. **Details of any sports interests or other pastimes such as music.**
8. **Details of any organisations you belong to.**
9. **It may also be useful to say if you have got a motorbike or bicycle or car since employers often prefer an applicant from nearby than one from farther away who would have to rely on public transport.**

Such a CV might end up looking like the one on page 134. Of course this is just an over-simplified example of a very basic CV for a school-leaver. In fact, your CV is an extremely important document, which is why we devote the whole of Part 3 of the book to them. See page 133 for the full information.

Send A Letter With It
All that is needed to accompany the CV is a short letter applying for the job. In this letter, say:

a) Which job you are applying for (there may be several advertised by big firms).
b) When you are available for interview and perhaps
c) Names, addresses and telephone numbers of referees who might speak up on your behalf.

Preferably type your letter; use a computer or word processor. Set out your name and address clearly at the top, check that you haven't let any spelling errors creep in, and type your name at the bottom, just below where you sign it.

If you are going to handwrite your letter, then the lay-out on the page should still be correct, with a proper margin on the left-hand side. Remember what you were taught at school about paragraphing. Do not cram your letter into a small space on the page, and try to keep the lines of your writing a uniform distance apart.

Make sure that your handwriting is easy to read, and if your spelling is poor, get someone else to check you have not made any mistakes.

Sign the letter at the bottom clearly, and print your name beneath your signature.

If there are only a few applicants for the job, the prospective employer will probably interview all of them. However, when there are a large number then he will 'weed' out the unsuitable ones just by looking at the letters. Your letter is, therefore, a vital part of getting an interview at all.

It is no use saying that you are 'applying for the job you have advertised'. You need to say just what job it is.

Say when you are available for interview, as it may cause some embarrassment if they ask you to attend at an inconvenient time.

Will It Really Suit Me?

Before you send the application off, make sure that you *really want* the job that you are applying for. You must have read carefully the advertisement or description of the job and you should already have talked it over with a person in a position to advise you.

Put this practical question to yourself: suppose the outcome of my application was favourable, would I have any doubt about accepting the offer?

If you appear to have any doubts at all at the interview, then this would prejudice the whole thing. You must have thought it through beforehand and arrive at the interview determined that you do want the job. Any half-heartedness may spoil your chances.

There is, nevertheless, a problem here that you may have to face. Suppose you have two or three applications out, and are called for interview for the one you regard the least favourably. What do you do? Take them into your confidence and say that if one of the others turns up you will accept it? (If you do, you risk being told not to bother to come.) Or ask for the interview to be postponed, hoping that you will hear good news from one of the others? (You *might* be lucky, but don't count on it.) Or go to the interview and accept the offer if it is made, with a mental reservation to cancel it if a better offer comes from elsewhere? (This is sometimes done, and you may regard it as a risk that people making appointments have to accept. How would you like it, though, if you were offered and accepted a place only to have the offer withdrawn later? In the last resort, only you can decide what to do when your interests and your sense of fairness pull different ways.)

Application Forms

In many instances, you apply for a job by filling in an application form rather than by writing a letter on your own initiative. Here is a check list of questions which you should ask yourself:

Have I filled in the application fully and accurately?
Are there any mis-spellings or faults of expression?
  If there are likely to be any of these, it is best to get a friend to look over a rough draft beforehand.
Is the handwriting easy to read?
  This is not a trivial question. Your application is an important document. You need to keep the reader on your side.
Are there any omissions to fill in, or revisions to make?
  There shouldn't be any if you gave proper attention to your rough draft. If you need to alter, do so boldly. Don't spoil the appearance of the application with smudged deletions or scrawled additions.

The most important part of your application form is

almost certainly the part in which you are free to write your own description of your career, interests, and supporting material.

Is this description in logical order?
Does it say all you want to say? And does it say it in a clear, fluent style, not breathlessly enthusiastic on the one hand, or terse and off-putting on the other?
Has it got any obvious omissions that will lead the reader to guess what you have left out, perhaps to your disadvantage?
Does it give most space to the important things, and less to the smaller details?
Have you used fully the space provided? If not, your interviewer will have to draw out further facts when he meets you, and he may feel that you have wasted some of his time in not setting them down in the first place.
Have you gone on to a further sheet if the application form invited you to do this? If so, make sure that the information on this sheet carries due weight; it is just as bad to be garrulous on paper as in conversation.

Sometimes you are expected to set out the whole of your application in your own way. This is a useful exercise in organizing clear, brief, factual statements. Set the facts out boldly, spacing them well, and underlining the headings. Your written application is your shop window. Dress it carefully, and don't be too modest about it!

You will find more information about application forms in 'How to prepare your application' (p. 73).

Answering Advertisements

The following advertisements form a representative sample of what you might see among others in the 'small ad.' SITUATIONS VACANT column of your local newspaper, together with some 'display ads.' of a similar type.

One or two of them invite you to send for details of the vacancies. In these cases you should do this before you send in a formal application or ask for an interview. When you

LEFT SCHOOL OR COLLEGE AND UNDECIDED WHAT TO DO?

We don't expect any young person to finally decide on the future before 25, that is why our training scheme for Junior Sales Executives is designed to give a thorough grounding in the operation of a modern, international manufacturing sales organisation, initially, with a strong bias towards Direct Selling to industry.

Salary commencing at up to £xxxx per annum (depending on age) with the chance to earn early increases. There are excellent opportunities for advancement into Field Sales and management at home or in South Africa, Canada, Australia and U.S.A.

Young people aged up to 23 should write or telephone for further details, quoting reference 2009.

TELEPHONIST

Person aged 21–40, required for National Daily Newspaper B.T. trained pref. £xx per week.

MACHINE ROOM MANAGER.

We are looking for a progressive Machine Room Manager to take full control of department in the small Litho Field. Applicants should be completely technical and have had previous control of running a department. Please write or phone.

ARE YOU AN EXPERIENCED GENERAL FOREMAN?

A GENERAL FOREMAN

(two posts) required to assist Site Supervisor in controlling contract for erection of Housing Association flats due to start in near future. Must have proven ability in this work and of handling all trades. Salary based on 40-hour week. Overtime as directed.

Appointment for duration of contract. Salary scale £xxxx to £xxxx.

INSURANCE CO. requires person age up to 30 years, experience in all aspects of Motor Claims to assist Head Office Motor Claims Superintendent in over-seeing Branch handling. The post offers a secure and progressive career. A generous salary, LVs and non-contributory Pension Scheme in respect of which consideration will be given to previous Insurance service.

A YOUNG PERSON with experience of order routine and some knowledge of paper and costing, required for internal printing department. Excellent conditions with assurance, pension and sickness scheme.

INVOICE CLERKS

Experienced invoice clerk, preferably with travel agency computer experience, required end of November for charge of invoice section of foreign touring office. Salary to £xxxx p.a. for the right person. Pension scheme. Also juniors. 19 plus, from £xx p.w., LVs.

We are a leading company in the field of specialised packaging products. Continuing expansion and diversification call for the appointment of a top-calibre person to the newly created position of Regional Sales Manager (South).

Experience of leading a small industrial sales team, together with the ability to negotiate at senior management level are essential requirements. A knowledge of the paper and/or packaging industries, while not essential, would be a distinct advantage. The successful candidate will be aged 30–45, and will preferably reside within easy access of Slough.

Commencing salary £xxxx plus bonus. Group contributory pension and life assurance schemes operate, and a company car is provided.

Write in confidence, with full personal and career details to the Sales Director.

send for details there is no need to say anything at all about yourself. You can make the request in a single sentence.

For example:

(Your address)
(Date)

Recruiting Officer,
OS/Word Processing,
Dept. of the Environment.

Dear Sir,

Please send me details of your word processing vacancies.

Yours faithfully,
(Your name)

In this case there is no need, either, to send a stamped, addressed envelope.

When advertisers invite applications from people who are qualified ('experienced', 'fully experienced', 'skilled', 'capable', 'first class') a list of exams passed, and relevant experience gained, must be given. But they often ask for other, and more general, qualities, such as 'intelligent', 'of good personality', 'with drive', 'responsible', etc. These are useful in telling the candidate the kind of questions that the employer might ask about him of a head teacher or other referee. There is nothing the candidate can do about them at the stage of seeking an interview, but he can be sure that he will be expected to give examples of drive and of responsibilities he has undertaken at the interview itself.

When you can offer an employer something which is not vital, but is a useful extra, it is worth mentioning this in your CV or preliminary letter, since the letters at this stage will probably be used to sift out the candidates. If you have been attracted by an advertisement which says 'some audio experience would be useful', or 'typing an advantage', or 'shorthand knowledge an asset', and you can offer something towards this 'extra', tell them so.

If the advertisement refers to training, express your willingness to accept this, but don't make a long story of it. An interviewer will often open his conversation with a candidate by referring to points made in the candidate's letter: 'From your letter you seem keen to start training . . .'

Sample Letters
A brief, fairly basic letter, asking for an interview for work in a general office, might be:

(Your address)
(Date)

Office Manager,

Dear Sir,

I am 16 years of age, and am due to leave Hillside Comprehensive School at the end of the summer term. I wish to apply for the vacancy in your general office advertised in last night's Leicester Mercury.

I can come for interview at any time out of school hours, or perhaps within school hours by arrangement with the Headmaster. I enclose some details about myself.

Yours faithfully,
(Your name)

A fuller letter, in reply to this advertisement

We have a vacancy for young person with minimum of 2 A-level passes who is interested in a worthwhile career in which full training is given. Please apply for interview to Branch Manager.

might take the following lines, if you were not sending a CV.

(Your address)
(Date)

Branch Manager.

Dear Sir,

I am interested in the vacancy you advertise for a

young person with a minimum of 2 A-levels.

I am 18 years of age, and am due to leave Shepstead 6th-Form College at the end of the Summer term. I already have 2 GCSEs at grade A, 2 at grade B and one at grade C, and am waiting to hear the result of two A-levels, one of which is in Mathematics, which I have a reasonable expectation of passing.

I have talked about a career in insurance with my uncle, who is an agent with an insurance company.

I am available for interview at any time, except for the week beginning June 26th, when I shall be engaged on a survey with a group from the school. You can contact me at home by telephone, if you wish. Our number is . . .

If you would like any further details about me before the interview, the Headmaster will be prepared to give them.

Yours faithfully,

(Your name)

Most straightforward jobs for those who leave school as soon as possible after they have reached school-leaving age are filled by personal application, either by turning up within the hours given in the advertisement, or by an appointment arranged over the telephone.

Some prospective employers may use the telephone conversation to make a preliminary assessment of you. Be ready. Think it out before you call. Be positive on the telephone and don't mumble. Know your qualifications and be sure you are really interested in the job. Otherwise you may find they tell you not to bother to come, particularly if they are trying to sift out those applicants for whom an interview would be a waste of time.

Such jobs might be advertised as follows:

'The Handyman' requires young person, aged 16–20 years, to train in the sales department, clean and tidy

appearance, good prospect of advancement. Apply to . . .

Grandisons require full-time assistant. Apply to . . .

As soon as you read advertisements like these in your local newspaper, you can probably picture the shops concerned, and have perhaps been inside as a customer. The second of the advertisements is very uninformative indeed, and it would certainly pay you to visit the premises before you thought seriously about applying. (What is the range of articles they sell? Does the shop give a good impression?)

'The Handyman' premises would be worth a visit too (unless you know them very well). Does the shop live up to the kind of salesman they hope to get? You might decide that it does, and be sufficiently attracted to apply.

Smaller firms would most commonly expect you to phone up to arrange a time for an interview, and you should do so as soon as you can after spotting the advertisement, otherwise the job may be gone! However, if it was a weekend or evening you might make a good impression by writing a letter like the one below and putting it through the letterbox:–

(Your address)
(Date)

'The Handyman'

Dear Sir,

I wish to apply for training as salesman in your shop. I am 16 years of age, and have just left . . . School. I think I can truthfully say that I am smart in appearance.

I think, too, that I would make a good salesman. I have sometimes helped out in a general store run by a friend of the family, and I have sold programmes, tickets, etc., for charities and various school events.

At school, I was in the top half of my class in most subjects, and passed three GCSEs at grade C and two at D.

I played regularly for the school in the Association Football League, and for my House at football and other sports.

In my last year at school I was a prefect, and carried out some duties in the library. I have made many things in the school workshops, and have helped to construct scenery for school plays. I have also done some do-it-yourself jobs at home.

I am available at any time, and look forward to hearing from you.

Yours faithfully,
(Your name)

This is not a long letter, but it is long enough to help the shop owner to make up his mind whether or not he would like to interview the writer. The young man has at least shown a practical interest in the two vital matters: selling, and being a handyman.

Need he have mentioned exam successes and his position in the class? Emphatically, yes. Rightly or wrongly, success in exams provides a stamp of quality in most employers' eyes. Probably rightly, because even in a practical situation like selling in a handyman's shop, academic successes prove that the applicant possesses versatility and personal resource that may be useful in many (and perhaps unexpected) ways.

Similarly, in an application for a 'bookish' job, success at sport or in a leisure pursuit proves that the candidate has a breadth of interest that may help him to adapt to changing circumstances in his job. In the course of time, jobs are bound to change, and the only kind of worker who is worth employing long-term is one who can cope with changes as they come.

As an example of an application for a 'bookish' job we might take a nationally-advertised vacancy in a Borough Treasurer's Department:

JUNIOR CLERK

Applicants with at least 3 higher grade GCSEs are invited for the above post which has excellent career prospects.

(Your address)
(Date)

Borough Treasurer.

Dear Sir,

I should be glad to be considered for the post of Junior Clerk in your Department.

I am 16, and have just left . . . School. The following are my GCSE subjects and grades: (There follows a neat table).

I took other, non-examination subjects as well, and was particularly interested in a General Course which included Social Studies.

I played a full part in school life, and have been Prefect, House Captain, and a regular member of the football and cricket teams. One of my proudest possessions is the bronze award of the Duke of Edinburgh's scheme. I am a strong swimmer, and have gained life saving and swimming certificates.

In my spare time, I am a motor cycle enthusiast, and a do-it-yourselfer. I also read a lot, and have contributed articles to the school magazine.

I am free to come for interview at any time.

Yours faithfully,
(Your name)

Personal Application

Most school leavers continue to live at home when they take their first job, so they naturally look for work a convenient travelling distance away. Since the work is near, it is equally natural for them to look the place over before they actually apply. When the advertisements say 'inquire', 'apply to', or even 'write or telephone', why not visit the office?

You might be seen on the spot by the person in charge

of filling the vacancy (though you would be lucky if this happened), but at least you could make arrangements for an interview.

Personal application, if you are successful in being seen at once, has the advantage of cutting down the period of waiting and worrying. If you are not seen on the spot, at least you have got a little of the 'feel' of the place. This is important, because so much of the anxiety of being interviewed is due to fear (if this is not too strong a term) of the unknown. The more you can learn beforehand, the less the unknown can worry you.

Do I Really Want Them?

One particular feature that you will be able to satisfy yourself about is the size of the concern. This may be mentioned in the advertisement itself ('a small company', for example, or 'a member of the . . . group of companies').

A small concern often has a happy, family atmosphere, in which everybody knows everybody else, and all are concerned with each other's welfare. Close contact between employer and employees may make for friendliness and reasonable efficiency. On the other hand, for the ambitious young worker, progress up the ladder may be blocked. A larger concern may have a good atmosphere too. The responsibilities and duties in it are likely to be more clear cut, and the ladder of promotion more open (and longer, too).

The size of the place you work in, like all the other features you look for, depends, in the end, on your personal preference, and, of course, on the availability of the kind of work you want.

One thing to avoid in a preliminary letter is asking those questions which should wait for the interview itself. This underlines the need, in your own interests, to go as well prepared as possible to interview.

Put very simply: the interview is the last occasion on which you are on anything approaching equal terms with your prospective employer.

3

Do They Mean Me?

When you read an advertisement for a job, take careful note of what the advertiser wants. Advertisements cost money, so an employer isn't going to pad out his description of a job with unnecessary words.

If, for example, you are attracted by an advertisement which calls for someone who is 'able to work without supervision', it is no use making an application which omits any reference to work which you have done on your own. At interview, you are bound to be asked about worthwhile work done either on your own initiative or with minimum guidance. You should go ready with samples of such work, which could be some do-it-yourself at home, a project at school, or a youth club venture in which your contribution fitted in with what other members did, or a hobby you have pursued.

Asked about work done without supervision, you might, in the course of conversation, say something like this: 'I can stick at a job until it's finished. I don't need to go running to someone else every five minutes to know how to go on. I find my own way round most problems, unless I can see that I'm wasting my time, or spoiling material, or something like that. Of course, I have to make sure I understand what's wanted in the first place, but once I've been shown, I pick it up pretty quickly'.

This sounds very good, but an employer may wonder

whether you stick at a job you set yourself, but wouldn't be wholehearted about one set by an employer. Some tasks are demanding and repetitive ones outside an applicant's personal interests. (One remedy for this lies with the employer: to see that work is as far as possible varied enough not to be an insult to a lively person's skill and intelligence.) An employer's doubts may be set at rest by examples of corporate effort, where the applicant has worked on his own to contribute to something that others have had a share in making too.

You can't make a long story of this in a written application, but a reference to work without supervision is worth a couple of sentences, or so. For example:

'In my last year at school I have done a number of things with little or no supervision. These include canvassing for advertisements for our school magazine, preparing models for demonstration at our annual exhibition, and the production of a folder on transport in our town for the GCSE exam.'

Interpersonal skills are another common theme in 'Situations Vacant' advertisements. Here is one of the variations: 'Able to deal with customer contact by letter and telephone'.

You might be able to say to your interviewer: 'I get on well with people, and have enough patience to hear them out. I catch on pretty quickly to what they are telling me, and can answer them briefly and to the point. I took a part-time job in a local store during the last summer holidays, and I think I served the public as cheerfully and efficiently as the full-time staff'.

In a written application there would be no need to refer to letter-writing because the application itself takes the form of a letter, but it would be useful if you could say 'I speak clearly, and my friends tell me that I have a good telephone manner'. When you write about your part-time job you might be able to mention that it involved some telephoning, even if it was only on an internal line. At least it would show acquaintance with the instrument.

The 'Cryptic' Advertiser
Some advertisers have a clear idea of their vacancies and of the people they hope will fill them, but the advertisements they publish are deliberately cryptic. What do you make of this?

> **'Are you a young person 16–18 looking for employment? Then perhaps you would like to train for a specific job of an interesting nature with prospects.'**

No other details are given, except for an address, a telephone number, and the office hours during which you may make your inquiries.

Employment agencies may advertise in this rather vague way, and so, sometimes, may firms with a number of openings, who hope that young people, attracted by curiosity, and by the words 'interesting', 'prospects' (or whatever other words are used) will apply.

Applicants risk wasting their time on these uninformative advertisements, but they may, on the other hand, gain from turning up at a place they wouldn't otherwise have considered for a job, to discover that the work, conditions, and atmosphere there are all just what they want. This underlines the fact that in job-hunting nothing can take the place of on-the-spot inquiry.

4

In The Waiting Room

You are almost certain to spend some time waiting, partly because some interviewers seem to delight in keeping people hanging around, but more importantly because:—
YOU HAVE GOT TO ARRIVE IN GOOD TIME.

Under no circumstances must you be late. After all a candidate who can't even manage to get to the interview on time is hardly likely to be a good time-keeper if he is given the job.

There is one problem you share with your interviewer: that of appearing bright and fresh at the start of the interview.

Whether this meeting with you is first or last on his list, you will expect your interviewer to be considerate in putting his questions and patient in hearing your answers.

You would be surprised, and annoyed, if others before you had worn him down, and so irritated him that he seemed anxious only to be rid of you.

You will find your session in the waiting room as wearing as he finds a succession of interviewees. As a rule, interviews are timed so that the waiting period is short. Even so, long waits are common and often harassing.

If you are waiting alone, the lack of human support may bring on a fit of nerves. If others are waiting with you, you may be shattered by their apparent confidence, their gossip – which always somehow suggests that they are 'in the know' and that you are an outsider – and their vast fund of experience.

Take it all with a pinch of salt. Others are as nervous as you are. Their 'confidence' may cover up a gnawing uncertainty. They may look assured because they are better actors than you are. Their chatter, and the experiences they exchange, may be a defence mechanism. They may fear drying up in the interview room, or stumbling in their speech, or saying foolish things, so they need to prove to themselves beforehand that they aren't like this at all.

Besides, what makes you think that nerves are a bad thing? They have a very useful function to perform – so long as you don't let them get on top of you. They are nature's way of mobilizing your resources for what is to come.

Sometimes, candidates wait gloomily with nothing said but the barest courtesies. If this is the situation you find when you are ushered in, you might as well conform. Any brightness you attempt will probably sound dreadfully hollow (though it is conceivable that the others may be grateful to you for livening things up).

Preliminary Thoughts

The best preliminary to your interview is to keep your mind active. You don't want to go in looking and feeling so inert that it takes all the interviewer's skill to rouse you. Keep yourself alert by running over some of the points you expect to come up in the space of your interview. (But don't worry at one particular point so long that you will be put off if the interview takes an unexpected turn and it doesn't come up at all.)

A quick round-up of points for the interview ensures that when your questioner raises them they will be in your recent memory, and you won't have to sit there tongue-tied while you try to dredge them up from the more distant past.

You might try to frame for yourself the kind of questions which will trigger the points off. Keep the questions simple, and your answers too.

Don't attempt to learn up answers to likely questions. If you do, you will probably produce a horrible, stilted, rehearsed effect. The facts, ideas, and comments you express are more important than the words in which you clothe them. Trust yourself, therefore, and follow the maxim: 'Take care of the sense, and the sounds will take care of themselves.'

Don't worry about the others

If the door to the interview room is solid and forbidding, and you can't hear a squeak of what is happening on the other side of it, don't let your imagination worry you sick with the idea that the candidate before you is getting a grilling, and that you will shortly be getting one too. Occupy yourself more profitably with your review of interview points.

Sometimes, though, you can hear the occasional burst of shared laughter from the room, or the soothing sound of normal conversation. This should put heart into you.

What are you to make of the candidates passing through the waiting room after their interview?

You will probably be reassured by their everyday appearance. They won't look as if they've had a shattering experience – and nor will you when your interview is over. You may even get from one of them the wink which says that the interviewer has proved unexpectedly human, and that the whole business wasn't so bad after all.

Even if a candidate comes out looking thoughtful, it probably only means that he had a question he meant to ask but when the opportunity came he couldn't for the life of him think what it was. It often happens that you only think of the really important questions when you've got outside the door.

5

What Makes A Good Interview?

A good interview will achieve 'rapport' between interviewer and candidate. They will find common ground, and go over it in a congenial atmosphere.

The candidate will leave the room with the feeling that he did himself justice, that he had ample opportunity to show his quality, and that his interviewer appreciated and approved that quality.

Even if, in the end, the candidate is turned down, he will have sufficient confidence in his interviewer to feel sure that the successful candidate must have deserved his success.

The interviewer, on his side, will feel that he has got the best out of each candidate, and probed deeply enough to make a decision that will stand the test of experience.

Everything depends on mutual trust. It is safe to say that your interviewer, whoever he is, regards himself as an open-minded, friendly person, anxious to give you the chance to show your paces. He is looking for the best possible candidate, and you may turn out to be the one who fits this description exactly.

You may gather a rather different impression of him. You may see him as self-important, and so ready to let fly with his opinions and criticism that he doesn't give you a chance. The very worst you could think of him is that the interview he conducted was a charade: that it was a foregone conclusion and that he never intended to accept you. (Sometimes this impression is due to listening too avidly to waiting-room gossip, and going into the interview convinced that the place was already promised to someone else. This could be part of the mythology of interviews, fostered so that disappointed candidates can put the blame for a poor performance on the interviewer rather than themselves.)

It is no use entering the interview room in a frame of mind that guarantees frustration for you. (Even if your interviewer is as bad as the worst you can think of him, you will at least gain useful experience, and your attitude to the situation may lead him to see merit in you that he did not expect.)

In a situation that you cannot control, the best thing you can do is to trust your interviewer, who might turn out less formidable than you expected. Your trust will nearly always be well placed. If you have prepared yourself properly for the experience (or ordeal, if you think of it that way) you will almost certainly be able to cope with whatever turns up.

There is one respect in which you may unwittingly do your interviewer an injustice. He is likely to receive you with cordiality to give you confidence and to get things moving smoothly. His manner, and the patient hearing he gives you, may suggest that he looks with special favour on your application. 'We got on like a house on fire!' might be your reaction.

But suppose you are rejected after all. Is your further reaction to be 'The two-faced so-and-so!'?

It shouldn't be. His cordiality is the same for others as for you. It is part of his style. Don't misinterpret it and end by thinking him a hypocrite.

Equally, if you are accepted, it is clear that you did a persuasive public relations job for yourself in convincing him of your merit. But don't imagine that his friendly manner might have told you that already. Interviewers don't give themselves away as easily as that.

Presenting Yourself

An interviewer nearly always has an interview sheet to fill in. He has it spread in front of him, and usually completes it unobtrusively. (You may find it rather daunting if he fills in the sheet about you with relish, or heavy breathing, or with much taking up and putting down of writing materials. Don't be too dismayed. He hasn't singled you out. He's like this with everyone, and if you keep your nerve your composure may lead him to write something to your credit. He might be doing this anyway.)

He probably has a line to complete on your appearance. What would you like him to put?

It's just as well to take stock well beforehand, and ask yourself what impression you want to create. Ask yourself, too, what impression you think you *do* create.

An interview is an important occasion – and not only for you. It is reasonable to expect candidates to be dressed appropriately. (One candidate turned up to an interview leading to professional training wearing rather rough working clothes. He defended his dress by saying that he wanted the interviewer to see him as he really was, and not dressed for the occasion. His attitude was laudable, no doubt, and his interviewer was duly glad that he had seen him 'as he really was'.)

Most candidates come to interview dressed in their best. I know that an interview is an artificial situation, and that when candidates dress up for it (and perhaps put on extra manners too, and make tongue-in-cheek claims about themselves and their experiences) the interviewer may have little idea of what they are like in a more everyday situation. But at least he knows that they are prepared to put themselves out in a situation of importance. An interviewer may deduce that if candidates are casual in dress they are probably casual in other things too. Correspondingly, if they take care of their appearance they may be just the careful people he is looking for.

A practical way of looking at how you should dress is this. Suppose you were successful at interview, how would you dress in the situation to which your application leads?

Dress for interview so as to look the part. A professional man should look like a professional man, a supervisor like a supervisor, etc. If you don't look the part, how can you expect people to take you seriously?

We all know that people of equal status, or in the same occupation, don't all dress alike. There must be some individuality too. This is where your temperament and taste come in. Do you want to stand out, or fit in? Are you a bit of an introvert, keeping yourself to yourself, and preferring to merge into the background rather than seek publicity? Either way, you can dress acceptably and still create the right image. If you are in any doubt at all, dress quietly and tidily so that you don't draw too much attention to yourself.

It may help you to look over this alphabetical list of words and phrases. Which would you like to be written against 'Appearance' on *your* interview sheet? Would it worry you if any of the others were used to describe you?

Colourless	Smart
Drab	Soberly dressed
Dressed in working clothes	Unkempt
Dressed to kill	Untidy
Fashionably dressed	Up-to-the-minute
Gimmicky	Well groomed
Neat	With-it
Over-dressed	
Presentable	

What gets written as a rule is factual and descriptive, but some terms imply criticism. Once it is written down, a critical description stands against you. You are not in a position to look over the interviewer's shoulder to see what he has put, so you are unable to defend yourself if you sense a bit of hostility.

Sometimes an interviewer will raise a question of appearance with a candidate:

'Is your hair always as long as this?'

'Weren't you able to tidy yourself up?'

'Have you come here straight from work?'

'I notice you bite your fingernails. Has this always been a habit of yours?'

He won't want to dwell on any of these things – and nor will you – but they help fill in the picture for him.

Structuring The Interview

No interview is exactly like any other. This is because no candidate is like any other.

An interview must be adaptable enough to meet the special needs of every interviewee, whoever he is. Yet it needn't be an aimless, gossipy chat. It has a serious purpose, and this can't be achieved unless there is a basic structure. Otherwise, comparisons could not properly be made, and the competitive element which is built into so many interviews would be plainly unfair.

The interviewer must ask all the questions necessary to form a rounded picture of each candidate, and to some extent these must be standardized. If the interview were too slavishly standardized, the information might just as well be got by means of a questionnaire (in this case, an extremely detailed application form).

An interview is really a compromise between a structured, standardized, the-same-for-all inquiry, and an open-ended conversation which is allowed to develop along lines basically indicated by the candidate himself. An interview which attempts to do justice to the candidate (and, don't forget, the needs of the organization to which he is applying) will start as the one and end as the other.

It doesn't follow that the interviewer gradually loses control. His role is to seek conclusions and to prevent drift. This is as much in the candidate's interest as his own. If the interview were allowed to fizzle out, both parties would share a dissatisfied feeling that the whole affair got nowhere, and the candidate would know that he had failed.

There is only one remedy for this situation: preparation by the candidate in presenting his case. He mustn't flop when the point arrives when the interviewer in effect says 'Over to you'.

The Right Impression

Don't count on your interviewer learning, by question and answer, all that he ought to know about you before he can make his decision. Make up your mind beforehand what, in your own interests, you want to tell him.

This extra information is vital. It rounds off your interviewer's total impression of you, and this is of greater importance than the skills that 'go with the job'. (What use would it be appointing a young person to help with the books simply because he was good at mathematics, if he was also dishonest, or a frequent absentee?) If the will to learn is there, the skills can be acquired with experience, but attitudes and outlooks can't be so easily changed. A young person might quite easily get taken on with less than the qualifications asked for if the interviewing employer feels 'I like the look of him', or 'He's a person after my own heart', or 'She's got something about her'.

Just what you've got about you may not be brought out in a conversation about the job unless you come prepared to express yourself.

A prospective employer (i.e. an employer from whom you are seeking a job) is bound to be interested in why you are applying for work in his particular field:

How long have you thought of taking up this kind of work?
Is your father (or brother, or any other relation) in a similar line?
Have you any friends doing this kind of work?
Do you know anyone who is working in the firm?

(A very useful pointer this; it suggests that you have talked it over with him, and that you already feel positively attracted by the work, or the firm, or both. It is also a useful pointer when two friends who have left school together seek work together.)

Why did you apply to work with us?

(If there are a number of openings in the locality it is interesting to an employer to know why you picked on him. Was it simply because his place of work is nearest to your home? Or because of his reputation as an employer? Or because he offers a good service or product to the public? Or did you apply to him because you hadn't bothered to find out what openings there were elsewhere? On the other hand, did you apply because of some personal recommendation you had? This last is, naturally, a strong card to play.)

Is this kind of work your first choice (or would you rather have done something else, and your hopes have been dashed)?

(It is obviously more attractive to an employer to take on someone who has chosen his kind of work in preference to any other. If the work comes a poor second to what the young worker really wants, the employer may fear that he may drift away if something apparently more attractive turns up. If you can say that the work you are applying for is genuinely what you want, this is clearly in your favour.

Some young people haven't a very realistic idea of what jobs are possible for them, and they may dream of 'glamour jobs'. A boy may be mad keen on football, but lack the talent that will turn him into the professional he would like to be. A girl may not have the figure or the poise to be a model or an air hostess. Commonsense in the end comes to the rescue of nearly all young people who live in a romantic dream-world, but an employer may notice what he thinks is a poor attitude in a boy or girl when the real cause is a sense of let-down, because the job hasn't the glamour he or she had hoped for.)

What have you done?
Your prospective employer will be interested to hear what subjects you did at school, how successful you were at

them, and which subjects you were really interested in. It will be much in your favour if your most successful, or your favourite, subjects lead naturally towards the kind of employment he can offer you. He may need to see proofs of success or achievement that you claim, in the shape of exam certificates or school reports. Have them ready in case he wants to see them.

A question at the back of your prospective employer's mind, though he may not ask it in this form (and perhaps he will not ask it at all) is this: 'What have you done at school, or in your spare time, that would help to convince me that you are the person I'm looking for? Can you give me any evidence to back up your application?'

Certificates and testimonials are one kind of evidence; and testimonials, although regarded with suspicion by some interviewers, are often important at the start of working life when you cannot demonstrate much experience. You may be able to use them to demonstrate application.

If you are a practical person, looking for a practical job, then bring along evidence of things you have made, or planned and carried out yourself. Some things can't be brought along, of course (for example, the fitment built into a room of your house), but a photo, accurate drawing, or sketch will show what you have done. Useful articles made in wood, metal, or other materials are a good guide to skill and interest. These may range from serviceable do-it-yourself to examples of genuine craftsmanship. The artistic is often as good a guide as the useful. I have seen paintings, pottery, musical instruments, dress designs, and many other things produced at interview. One effect of showing a wider range of things at interview is to prove that a girl who is 'good with her hands' is not necessarily lacking in ideas or imagination too – and the same goes for the boy.

What Is The Interview Really For?

Never forget that an interview is not just a conversation about work between an employer and a prospective employee. All the time the conversation is going on, the employer is trying to picture the applicant in the job they are talking about.

When you come up for interview, the employer will have this advantage (among others) over you: he knows all the duties that go with the job, and all the demands it would make on you, if he appointed you. How can you convince him that you could cope with it?

There are several answers to this question.

You wouldn't have applied in the first place if you hadn't some idea what the work entails, and could picture yourself doing it. You know whether it needs strength, or some physical skill that you possess and could develop, or good eyesight and attention to detail, or the capacity to stand doing repetitive movements; you know whether it is indoors or out, and whether it involves travel; you know, too, whether it involves meeting people, particularly the public.

A job that needs strength or stamina calls for a good health record, in which case you will be ready with details of health and things you have done that prove your fitness. For a job that calls for mechanical sense you will need to show your acquaintance with machinery, perhaps through driving, or car or motor cycle repair and maintenance.

Work in a shop will include duties which must be done with care, courtesy, and accuracy. Can you handle goods without being clumsy? Can you listen patiently to a member of the public explaining what she wants, and help her to find it, or perhaps a near alternative, in the shop? Could you take money and give change throughout a day and be able to account for it all at the end? Can you take orders from a superior, even if you don't always see the point of them? Does your experience in school, at home, or in a shop as a customer, throw any light on how you would take to shop work? If so, speak out at your interview.

Work as a secretary or receptionist demands neatness and good organization, and the capacity to write or type businesslike letters and to use the telephone. Can you do all these things? If you made a written application, you certainly proved whether you can write a good letter, but what about the other things? I have known a girl with quite a lot to commend her lose the chance of a secretarial job because her prospective employer asked himself at her interview 'What would a member of the public make of her at the other end of a telephone line?'

If applicants lack the physical or technical skills necessary for a job, they simply don't put in for it. They know from their health or sports record at school, or from poor exam results what they are lacking, and they can't very well deceive themselves that they possess what is wanted.

Try A Bit Of Self-criticism

But social skills aren't examined or tested in the same way, so there is plenty of scope for an applicant to put in for a job that really wouldn't suit. He (or she) must test himself for smartness (if this is called for in a job), or the ability to meet members of the public in a helpful and relaxed way, or the ability to write a letter of information, advice, or complaint, or the ability to use a phone. If you can't be self-critical, you are not yet ready to put in an application which an employer can take seriously.

Self-criticism is all very well, but what are you to do about the failings you see in yourself? On the way you present yourself, for example. There are plenty of newspapers and magazines (as well as parents and friends) free with advice on good grooming and dressing well. The important thing is to choose a style which suits yourself, and unless you are very discriminating you may need to seek a friend's helpful opinion.

Many young people dress smartly, yet give themselves away when they open their mouths. This is not to suggest that you, as a candidate for a job, have got to speak with a put-on BBC newsreader's accent, but that you drop any rough, slangy speech that may go down well enough among friends, and make a conscious effort to speak clearly in an adult way.

If the job calls for meeting the public, why not visit

shops, showrooms, and other places where salespeople and officials actually meet the public, and exercise your capacity for appreciation and criticism on what you see and hear? Whom, among those you observe, would you like to model yourself on? Who is an 'awful warning'?

The courtesy, patience, tolerance, ability to listen, and other qualities shown by people on the job already will also be expected of you. If you can learn to suppress faults in yourself in time for your first meeting with your prospective employer, and can bring out the personal relationships you can already manage quite well, you are likely to do better than the candidate who comes along hoping to 'play it all by ear'.

As for using a telephone, and sounding like a responsible adult to the person at the other end of the line, there is only one recipe for success, and that is experience. Ring up a friend. What is your friend's candid opinion of your performance? If your friend is at all critical, is it possible that the same criticisms might apply to your performance at interview? If so, the remedy is obvious – isn't it?

All this is part of the process of helping your prospective employer to picture you in the job for which you are applying. There are other ways too.

Know Where You Are Going

The most convincing way of showing that you are fit for a job is to be able to prove (if you can) that you've already done a similar kind of job in the form of part-time or holiday work.

In this respect, it is an immense advantage to know, well before you leave school, what kind of full-time work you will eventually seek. This should help you to choose the kind of part-time work that will show whether you have a genuine taste or aptitude for it. Even if your part-time work lies in a different field, it will reveal a lot about yourself, from a simple fact like whether you can get up in time to get to work punctually, to facts like whether you possess the qualities the job demands.

If you can speak with knowledge and enthusiasm about

a part-time job you have done successfully, you will have an advantage over an applicant whose capacity to work is an unknown quantity. Moreover, you will be able to use your part-time employer as a referee (with his permission, of course) in applying for full-time employment.

Whatever the job, you will need a period of getting to learn the hang of it. With some jobs, there is a period of training; with others, you learn the job by doing it, under the care of some experienced person. Whether the period of training is long or short, with a spell under a supervisor before you are on your own, express your willingness and interest in learning to do the job properly. Don't ever make the mistake of turning down offers of help, or give the impression that you think that you know it all from the start.

A good way of expressing your interest, and informing yourself at the same time, is to find out what you can about the firm beforehand. Perhaps you can call and look round. Perhaps you can discover the firm's local reputation and the scope of its activities. Perhaps you can chat with an employee and get an 'inside' view of the job before you really commit yourself to it. (Don't forget, though, that an employee sometimes takes a very prejudiced view of the firm he works for. If he is disgruntled about something you may not be able to take what he says very seriously. If he expresses warm feelings towards his firm this should encourage you. In this case, it would be well to mention it at interview that you know something about the firm already, and that you have spoken to an employee who is very satisfied to work for it.)

Attitudes

However carefully you match what you think a job requires with what you have to offer, there is always something further that you bring to it. You can call this rather grandly your philosophy of life, or you can come down to earth and call it your attitude to work.

The longer your interview, the more surely your attitude will show itself (and the more surely your employer will know whether or not he has picked the right person). If you see work as simply what has to be gone through to provide a wage packet at the end of the week, you are not likely to put your heart into the job. Your prospective employer might then suspect you of being a possible slacker and frequent absentee, and altogether a poor risk.

In fact, though, most people do not put money at the top of the list of what they expect from work. Workpeople – and probably you too – are more likely to put job satisfaction and working among friends at the top of the list.

It is reasonable, though, to look for a combination of things you most value in a job, and it would be a poor interviewer who did not discover something about these things in his conversation with you. You will not be surprised if he draws his own deductions from what he finds out.

Different Types Of Interviewer

If you apply for a job with a small firm, you can expect your interviewer to be shrewd, with an intimate knowledge of the firm's needs. He may be the proprietor himself, or a manager on whom the proprietor relies. He will know, from personal acquaintance, about the careers of others who have served with the firm, and know who turned out to be good appointments, and the few whose appointment turned out to be a mistake. He will know what kind of person the success of the firm depends on, whether that person makes important decisions or simply fits in well with the firm's particular way of doing things. Unless the firm has a high turnover of staff – a bad sign – an interview will be a fairly rare event.

An interviewer with a large concern (firm, college, local authority, for example) will be kept busier and use methods which are better structured than those used by the small concern. In the technical sense he may well be more 'efficient' but he is likely to have just as many failures as the proprietor of the village shop.

An interview with a small firm is likely to be more

chatty and informal than one with a large firm, and you are likely to feel more confident and relaxed because of this, but the need to present yourself well is at least as great in this situation as in the other.

Discussing The Terms
One thing almost certain to be discussed is what your pay would be, if appointed. Large Companies and Local Authorities or Government Departments generally have fixed rates of pay which may vary for different grades according to experience, qualifications or assessments. If so, the rate of pay will often have appeared in the advertisement and you would not have applied for the job unless it was acceptable.

With smaller employers the rate of pay may be a matter for negotiation and you should have a clear idea (from friends or even parents) of what to expect – you might even be asked how much you are expecting by the employer! Never expect to get exactly the same wages as your friends – teenage employees should get rises from time to time anyway – but nevertheless if you are offered something well below the going rate, you should be ready to provide chapter and verse examples of pay in similar occupations for people of your own age. No sense in being exploited.

Pay isn't everything. You need to know what else goes with the job. Employment is quite often a 'package deal' with extras thrown in, or inducements offered to the worker to keep down the cost of taking the job. These can be quite substantial; they are also very varied.

Here are some of them: a house that goes with the job; removal expenses to persuade an employee to move to the area of his new work; lodging expenses where the employee has to go away for training; the use of a car (perhaps with private use allowed at week-ends and holidays), or a mileage allowance for the use of the worker's own car; free transport to work and back again; a uniform, or special clothing, or money in lieu; a mid-day meal free to the worker, or subsidized; the right to buy, cheaper than the public can, goods or services produced by the firm; sports facilities, welfare services, etc. 'Perks' include special bonuses or benefits that might be given at Christmas or other times of the year, and the amount of paid holiday that is allowed.

'Perks', in fact, are all those rights which a worker enjoys because he is an employee of a firm or other body. They should be discussed fully at the same time as pay and conditions.

A worker likes to feel that he is looked after by whoever employs him, and correspondingly an employer likes to be regarded as a 'good employer'; in practical terms, this helps to create loyalty among his staff.

It is worth bearing in mind that what seems to the outsider as a very attractive rate of pay sometimes conceals poor conditions of work. (Workers wouldn't accept conditions like that if the pay weren't good.)

When pay seems to be a bit low, so that you might wonder why workers don't drift off into jobs with a bigger pay packet, the explanation may be that 'perks' tip the balance.

In small concerns, the whole 'package' is settled by direct negotiation between employer and employee. With the bigger concern, pay, conditions, etc., may be settled by employers and Trades Unions.

Employers and employees want the best bargain they can make with each other. When the employer offers a particular wage for a job it might not be his last word. Would he pay a higher wage if pressed? What is the prospective employee's bargaining position? What is the bargaining position of someone straight from school who may not know the ins and outs of the labour market?

This last question really answers itself: if a recent school-leaver doesn't know the labour situation he isn't in a position to bargain.

Wages depend very much on what is customary in the area. If a newsagent needs another delivery boy, he will expect to pay him what he paid the last one; if a shop-keeper needs an assistant, he will expect to pay the same as he pays other assistants, or what he knows other shop-keepers are paying. When labour of the right sort or quality is scarce, an employer may have to pay higher wages; when there are more workers than jobs, he can recruit them at the usual wages, or even a little less.

People talk, and compare notes, so any changes in the job situation soon become known, and people tend to move off to where pay and conditions are better, unless they have special reasons for staying where they are at the old rates.

Those who have just left school need to discover what rates and conditions are possible in the range of jobs they are willing to undertake. If you are a school-leaver, this information will tell you whether or not you are bargaining from a position of strength. It's as well to know!

A Summary Of Advice
1. Be ready with all the basic facts about yourself (particularly education, experience, interests, sport, hobbies) that an employer is likely to ask about. Be ready, too, with all the explanations you might be asked to give (the 'how' and 'why' as well as 'what' and 'when'). If you can show that your education, experience, and various activities lead naturally to the kind of employment he has to offer, this is a strong recommendation.
2. Back up your application with tangible evidence if you can, and by referring to any part-time work you have done.
3. Show a genuine interest in the work, and in the firm you have applied to. Part of the proof of this interest is the trouble you have taken to inform yourself about the work and the firm.
4. Try to analyse, as far as you can, the kind of skills and qualities demanded by the work, and see how far your own skills and qualities match these demands. Apart from training in the work, which you can expect the firm to give, see whether you can discover your own short-comings and remedy them.

5. When you come to interview try to look, speak, and act as the kind of person your prospective employer is looking for. If you can do all this, and still be natural, you will stand a better chance of being accepted. After all, you have left school (or are shortly to leave) and now is your chance to show yourself as a responsible adult.

6

How To Approach That Test

Candidates for entry into occupations involving practical skill are often asked to undergo a test. This may be anything from a well-established test of aptitude used by a large concern, down to a brief test of know-what and know-how devised and applied by a small employer.

An aptitude test is basically one of practical intelligence. It may test your knowledge, your capacity to 'see through' to the heart of a problem, your ability to understand relationships in a practical setting, the skill of your hands, your observation and attention to detail, your capacity to experiment until you have found the 'right' or the most promising solution, and other qualities bound up with these.

It may include any or all of the following, and more besides:

> 'pencil and paper' tests, rather like intelligence tests and quizzes, but in a practical setting,
> the observation of mechanisms and answering questions about them,
> the assembly of simple mechanisms,
> explanations of how things work,
> the manipulation of wooden blocks, patterned cards, and other test material according to instructions.

These tests may have to be done against the stop-watch.

An aptitude test may include items that might not seem very practical to you, but are designed to discover background knowledge and interests. There is a close tie-up ('correlation') between knowledge, interest, and aptitude.

Aptitude tests reveal qualities which are valuable in a particular kind of job, but they also protect some individuals from undertaking a job they are not really fitted for. It is better to fail such a test, and suffer disappointment before they are committed to the job, than to discover, on the job itself, that they are round pegs in square holes. Aptitude tests are very good at cutting down the number of misfits.

If you have to take an aptitude test, you won't want to throw away your chances by adopting the wrong approach to it.

Commonsense tells you that you should follow all the instructions carefully, and go ahead in a confident and relaxed (but not casual) manner. Experience of tests, however, suggests further, and more detailed advice.

Never under-rate a test, however simple it seems. Every worth-while test has been tried out and checked until we can be sure that there is point and purpose in every item, and that the results given by the test as a whole tally reasonably well with experience.

Easy items help to build confidence and to show the candidate what is expected of him.

I have seen what happens when people scorn the easier items in a graded test, and come in at a later stage, only to find that the later items were harder than they had supposed. Doing the easier items would have helped them to get the hang of the test as a whole.

Don't be worried about failing parts of a test. What would be the point of a test which was so easy that failure was ruled out? It wouldn't really test you at all. Nobody will ever know what you are capable of until you have been brought to the point where you begin to fail.

What interests the tester is where this point comes.

What may interest him still more is your attitude to difficulties. Are you easily rattled? Do you keep trying the same wrong approach as if you expect that sheer repetition will turn it into the right one? Have you enough resource to see alternative methods and try them out? Do your attempts suggest that you appreciate the nature of the difficulty that's holding you up? Are you so absorbed in tackling a difficult item that you spend too long on it and get impatient and annoyed, and feel that your personal pride is being damaged? Not all tests are against time; when they are, there are occasions when it is better to drop an unsatisfactory item than to persist with it.

Be systematic. In aptitude tests which involve practical equipment (assembling mechanisms, for example) take plenty of space, keep together all those things that go together, and don't get in a muddle as you move things around.

Don't be too cautious. Sometimes a candidate tackles an easy item ultra-cautiously, because he thinks it can't be as easy as all that. He suspects a trap.

Be reassured. Nearly all tests are perfectly straightforward, in the sense that the candidate knows clearly what is expected of him, even if he cannot do it.

7

The Brighter Side

Suppose You Don't Land The Job You Want

Do you expect to land the first job you apply for? You will be lucky if you do! It would be like looking in the window of a shop and seeing exactly what you want straight away. It's good advice to 'shop around'.

You, as a younger worker, will shop around for a job that suits you, and employers will 'test the market' (which amounts to the same thing) by seeing a number of applicants and choosing the best.

It's no reflection on you if you aren't picked first time. It might be to your advantage to be turned down, if you have been a bit lazy and not taken the trouble to discover the extent of the market for what you can offer. Being turned down will make you look around. It will also tell you – if you don't know it already – that it doesn't pay to be too choosy, particularly when jobs are scarce.

If you get as far as an interview for the first job you apply for, and are turned down, at least you will carry away a useful experience. You will know how you were received, and how you perhaps felt a bit inadequate and floored by some of the questions put to you.

Treat it, then, as a warm-up for the next interview – the one that matters. Don't imagine, though, that the second will follow exactly the lines of the first. Employers are individualists, and though the basic questions will be the same, the follow-up questions will probably not be. So don't be disheartened by your 'failure' at the first interview, nor over-confident at the second because you think you have got the measure of the situation.

As a school-leaver, you come on to the labour market along with a great many others. At certain times of the year there is a flood of new job hunters. It is a very competitive situation, and it will be a shattering experience for those who put themselves forward with high hopes and expectations, and are turned down at a series of interviews, if indeed their applications reach the interview stage.

There comes a time for many young people, particularly when there is high unemployment, when they must sit down and take stock of the real 'outside world' situation.

First, are you really sure where your strengths lie? If so, it is best to wait until you have exhausted all the local possibilities of employment in your chosen field before you panic.

Take advice from friends, relatives and officials who, between them, know local conditions better than you do. Getting the right kind of job may depend, in the end, on how mobile you are. How far are you prepared to travel, day in, day out, to a job? Are you willing, if necessary, to leave home?

When unemployment is high and there is no job to be found, here are three possibilities you should examine before you take to the dole queue.

First: You might stay on at school for another year (or two years), not just in the hope that 'things will improve' but with a view to improving your education and qualifications. At the same time you may be able to get part-time evening, weekend or holiday jobs to improve your 'track record'.

Second: If you have been turned down for lack of some particular qualification you may be able to fill the gap at College. Get advice from the Careers Office.

Third: School-leavers in the UK can apply to go on one of a number of training schemes or initiatives, which may combine Further Education with practical work experience. Again, Careers Officers can give details.

This may sound like defeatism, but it isn't really. You may, like many others, have left it until rather late in your school career to decide what you really want to do. If so, you may wish you had studied some particular subject more attentively, or to greater depth. Now would be the time to fill any gaps. This course of action may be the best for you, but seek advice first, from those best qualified to give it.

You will naturally talk to others in similar circumstances to yours. You will have to use your own discretion if you are told by a friend (as you might quite well be) that he got fed up with learning and wouldn't go back to school or on to College at any price.

Do You Really Want The Job?

Believe it or not, some candidates who come up for interview don't really want the jobs they have applied for. Some of the others are so half-hearted that they leave it to the interviewer, as a kind of umpire, to make the decision for them. If accepted, they may go ahead with a good heart, and eventually make a success of the job; or they may stick it for a time, and then drift off again.

All this can come about for a variety of reasons. Sometimes, serious doubts arise in a candidate's mind after he has sent off his application. He hasn't resolved them by the time he comes up for interview. He doesn't want to spoil his chances by refusing the job, in case he finally decides to go forward. He leaves his options open – at least for a time.

Some candidates with doubts are the sort who find it hard to make decisions about important things. Basically, they can't face the blame if things go wrong. They are all right in uncomplicated everyday matters, but vital decisions, with consequences that can't be fully known, are a worry and embarrassment to them. They privately heave

65

a sigh of relief whichever way the interviewer's decision goes.

Some candidates can't make up their minds because they don't know whom to consult (or whom they can trust). They may fear to disclose their private ideas or ambitions to anyone in case they are frowned on or laughed at. They may feel that the advice given is only what the adviser is paid (or expected) to give, and isn't really tailored to the candidate's individual needs. They may feel that the adviser hasn't the time, or doesn't know enough, to go into the candidate's prospects, with alternatives, in such a way as to carry conviction with the candidate – who is the person who really matters.

On the face of it, a candidate ought to have plenty of advice to go on, with lots of practical knowledge thrown in, from his potential battery of helpers, who may include parents and relations, schoolmasters, friends (including boy- or girl-friends), and official careers and employment officers.

You can add, also, the person-to-person advice that may come from training and personnel officers of firms and officials of organizations whom the candidate may contact, as well as that readily available in books, pamphlets, journals, newspapers and advertisements.

Despite all the help available, some candidates apply for a job, not as the result of a rational decision, but because, for some reason, they have been swept into it by forces they can't control. Many of these candidates are young people who have had the job wished on them, perhaps by parents. They haven't the strength of will to say 'No', and perhaps rely on the interviewer saying 'No' for them.

Some are in this position not because of the machinations of well-meaning parents and friends, or because they lack the will to make a responsible choice for themselves, but because they have left decision-making too late. They need a personal campaign to find and assess the facts well in advance of the critical decision.

8

Your Second Job

How does an interview for your second job differ from the interview for your first? When you come up for your second job you will be older and more experienced than when you were a raw recruit for your first. You can expect a good deal of questioning on your experience in your first job, your reasons for leaving it, and your reasons for your new application. A good deal may depend on the length of time you were employed in your first job.

If this turned out to be a dead end, no one would be surprised at your wanting to leave. A young worker with enthusiasm and personal resource has every right to leave a job which has no prospects as soon as a better one turns up. But what about a worker in a progressive job which offers chances of promotion to more interesting and responsible work? If he leaves this one without giving it much of a trial, a new employer may suspect that he is a bit work-shy and unwilling to accept responsibility.

It is a good general rule to stay long enough at a job at least to give it a fair trial. If it is a job with prospects, in a good firm, you may decide to stay with it. If you do decide to leave, be clear yourself what your reasons for leaving are. They are bound to be asked when you want to start somewhere else.

Reasons vary a great deal. Marriage and prospects of marriage play an important part for some young people.

(E.g. wanting to be near boy- or girl-friend, or near the home young marrieds have set up together.) Gaining wider or different experience is another reason, and so is the wish to join a larger firm, or to start out independently. It is up to the individual whether he really wants to move. To stay too long may label him unambitious, or a dull stick-in-the-mud.

However good his reasons for leaving, he should beware of too many moves in a short period. This may alert a prospective employer to the fact that he might be a drifter, who will drift away from him as he has drifted before, so that the employer sees little return from any training he gives him.

Checklist for School-Leavers

1. *Choosing a career*
   Have you considered all the possibilities, and discussed them with parents, teachers and Careers Officers?
   Have you made sure that your choices are possible on the basis of the qualifications you have got or expect to get?
2. *Looking for a job*
   Check newspaper and shop window advertisements every day.
   Keep in constant contact with the Careers Office.
   Call on likely employers even if no job advertised.
   Keep asking friends who are in work whether there are any vacancies.
   Have your referees, exam certificates and testimonials ready all the time.
   Have your CV ready.
   Get evening or Saturday jobs to improve your track record.
   Apply for all jobs you like the look of.
3. *Preparing for an interview*
   Be on time or early.
   Dress neatly and put on your best appearance.
   Consider and have a good idea of what wages you expect.
4. *During the interview*
   Be positive – know what you want.
   Be ready with the basic facts about yourself.
   Know why you've applied for that particular job.
   Look, speak and act like the kind of person the employer is looking for.

Part 2

Here we deal with more sophisticated job-hunting.

9

How To Prepare Your Application

Your application may be made in one of two forms, either (a) you are going to be writing a letter, which you will probably attach to your CV, or (b) you will have to fill in an application form, which you may or may not attach to your CV.

The Letter
Make brief jottings on what you expect to include. Cover and check important matters, especially things which are not covered in your CV. It is worth taking time over this and maybe it should be looked at on several different days. If possible, put it up on a computer or word processor. Then you can alter it easily.

Turn it into a proper draft, stressing the account of yourself and what you have to offer. See how it reads, whether it is sensibly organized, and perhaps how a reader is likely to take it.

Once you are happy with it, print it off and put it in front of someone you can trust for his comments. Pay heed to his comments, but don't necessarily follow his advice slavishly.

If you are making several applications around the same time, you can save effort and possibly improve presentation by having a general letter on the word processor or computer which you can alter around to suit the different people you are applying to.

If you have not got access to a word processor or computer, and you have to do it just by hand or typewriter, rough it out first in your own hand, then type it out in a rough draft to show to someone else, and then *take very great care indeed* to produce a perfect final version, making sure that there are no mistakes or corrections in what you actually send.

The Application Form

Fill it in carefully. This may sound like a blinding glimpse of the obvious, yet I frequently see errors.

If your handwriting is notoriously bad, you must at least make the effort to write legibly on this important occasion. But don't write such a painstakingly careful hand that all individuality is drained out of it.

You can use a typewriter to fill in the form, unless the application is asked for 'in the candidate's own handwriting'. Some people believe that handwriting gives a clue to character, and you must go along with this in this respect, whatever your private feelings.

Where you are allowed to type, you can type out the draft on plain paper, double spaced, to leave plenty of room for amendment. Then re-check it and think about it for a day or two, before typing it out single spaced, again on plain paper, to make sure it fits. Then, after any further necessary adjustment, you can type it on the form.

Then give the whole form a very careful check.

Remember that the reason why they have given you an application form is because they want it filled in so that they can compare one with another. It is, therefore, on the whole inadvisable to put 'See CV' in the spaces on the form, as this will involve the reader in extra effort to understand your application. Be guided on this, though, by the instructions on the form.

Anyway, you should attach your CV or Résumé to the form before sending it off.

Some people work themselves into an agony of doubt before sending in an application. You might think, before sending in your own application, that part of it might be better expressed. Perhaps it might be, but unless something positively cries out for correction it is better to leave it as it is.

In application forms it is common to ask:
Surname and forenames; address, telephone number
Date of birth
Marital status
Number and ages of children
Parent, Guardian, or next-of-kin, with address, telephone number
Nationality
Religion. (This is occasionally asked. Don't be alarmed by the question. It may be asked for severely practical reasons, e.g. it is well to know when religious observances are likely to take the applicant from his work.)
Questions about health. (Usually very general, but specific when it comes to disabilities which might affect employment.)
Details of education and qualifications. (Including future plans and exams still to be taken.)
Details of employment. (Including reasons for leaving jobs you have had, and your reasons for leaving your present job; including duties and responsibilities in your present job, your present pay, and perhaps pay in previous jobs; your reasons for making this particular application.)
Details of interests of all kinds
References
Questions about: how you learned of the firm you hope to join,
relatives employed by the firm,
previous employment in the firm or firms within the same group,
service in HM Forces, etc.

You may regard a question on 'Pay required . . .' as rather a sticky one. Bear in mind that the pay you expect should be a logical continuation of what you have received so far. The higher the pay you claim, the more searching you can expect your prospective employer to be in questions of qualifications and relevant experience. You could very well state a range of pay, so that the employer would understand that the actual pay is negotiable within that range.

An application form is a confidential document. This is usually specifically stated (perhaps in the section dealing with present employment, where it may say that the employer will not be contacted unless the applicant has been interviewed. This saves the applicant the embarrassment of letting his employer know that he is seeking a job elsewhere).

Some forms are neatly-designed all-purpose documents. They include all the basic facts about the applicant, and all those things a company or other body needs to know before accepting him. They include, also, spaces for notes and assessments made about him at interview, as well as spaces for checking all the necessary details of accepting him as employee, student, etc.

Such forms are easily filed, and can be quickly referred to in case of query or dispute. The candidate will probably not understand the cryptic (to the outsider) coding of details of receiving him into the firm or organization, but he does have a chance of seeing how much space is allotted to interview notes and assessments, and can therefore to some extent gauge its importance.

The all-purpose nature of such forms sometimes makes the applicant wonder why on earth they want to know all the information they seek. In one part of the form, he fills in the line which asks him what kind of appointment he is looking for, and in another he is asked whether he speaks a foreign language (and if so, how well), and whether he holds a driving licence. Perhaps his preferred employment demands neither.

It is just as well to complete the form fully. Jobs change,

and new opportunities come up and are offered to those in a position to grasp them. If you have applied for a particular job which turns out not to be open to you, your application may stay in the files until a similar one comes along. If your application was a general one, asking for appointment whenever a suitable vacancy occurs, the more information you can give the better. This advice is reinforced by the fact that forms sometimes ask what other work you are able to do. (Don't say 'Any'. This is too vague. It couldn't be true, anyhow. Be as specific as you can.)

Some application forms are rounded off in the simplest possible way with the date and signature of the applicant. The applicant has given his information, and the signature testifies to its correctness.

Sometimes this is put formally: 'I hereby certify that the answers given are true to the best of my belief' (or words to that effect). Occasionally, this is extended to include a declaration that the applicant has not withheld any information which might be to his disadvantage.

References And Testimonials
References are different from testimonials but people sometimes confuse them.

A *reference* is confidential. When you leave a job it is sensible (if you have done well there) to ask your employer if you can give his name as a reference – and this means that new employers to whom you apply may contact the referee to find out things about you.

A *testimonial* is of less value. It is often a typewritten sheet of paper given by the employer to someone who is leaving – which can then be shown to other potential employers.

References
You probably have to give the names of one or two referees with your application. Whom do you ask to act for you?

It must be someone who knows you well enough to be

able to give reliable help to whomever deals with your application. It must also be someone of good standing who can give an unprejudiced appraisal of you.

It is no use having as referee a friend who will stick up for you come what may, so that his praise may be suspect, particularly if the reader of his reference has cause to wonder whether some damaging facts have been omitted or glossed over. If the reader does not find the information he expects in a reference, he may 'read between the lines' and suspect that it is not there because it would not support your case.

A reference with too many superlatives is unlikely to be balanced enough to be really helpful; if it is too critical, it might spoil your chances. The best kind of reference is one which the reader feels to be frank and balanced, so that any criticisms are offset by positive recommendations which carry conviction.

The reader will want to know how long your referee has known you – and how recently. His reference wouldn't be much use if he knew you ten years ago but has since lost touch with you.

This raises a practical matter for you. Never use a person's name as a referee without his permission. If you put in several applications shortly after getting his agreement, there is no reason why you should not use his name for all of them. But if some time elapses between one round of applications and the next, it is as well to express your thanks and ask him to renew his permission.

It is a small thing for you to give a person's name and address on your application and then sit back and await developments. To a referee it can be a bit of a chore if he is asked for a reference at a particularly busy time.

He won't want to handicap you by failing to answer, or by delaying his answer so that it doesn't arrive in time. If he is interested enough in you to back your application, you can at least tell him the eventual outcome. (Be cautious about ringing him up to discover whether he has been asked for a reference. Understandably, you are on tenterhooks wondering whether you will be called to interview.

But unless you know your referee *very* well, he may feel that these demands on his attention are getting too much, and begin to regret that he ever undertook that task at all.)

It is quite possible that the person who considers your application will not only ask for a reference, but follow-up with a telephone call to your referee to fill in any gaps or answer a few queries. This may be necessary so that the interviewer is as fully informed as possible by the time he meets you.

Testimonials

For the same reason, your interviewer may ring up the writer of a testimonial. (Never send an original, *always* a copy.)

Testimonials have two disadvantages from the point of view of an interviewer: they date, and they are seen by the applicant. The interviewer may wonder whether anything has happened since a testimonial was written to cause the writer to change his mind about you, or whether there are fresh facts that he would add if he were writing it now. (You can help yourself here by asking the writer of an old testimonial to re-date it, or revise it, before you send a copy with your application. Testimonials over five years old are probably of doubtful value. In the course of time, as you gather fresh experience, they are superseded by more up-to-date ones.)

References are confidential, and therefore more candid than testimonials. The writers of both are probably just as honest as one another, but the writers of testimonials are likely to spare themselves embarrassment about referring to one's limitations by tactful omissions.

Testimonials are rather general, and can be used in whatever way the applicant thinks fit. References, on the other hand, are specific. The referee is given details of the particular appointment or place that the applicant is seeking, so he knows the context in which his reference will be used. There is an advantage to an applicant here, because the referee can emphasize qualities and skills that are appropriate in this context.

10

The Interview Itself

All interviews differ in style and approach. The following suggestions are by no means exhaustive but provide a framework which *might* be experienced.

Some things for you to bear in mind	Some things your interviewer is thinking about

1. The courtesies

It helps you to know your interviewer by name. He is a person too! If he is the right man for this kind of job, his warmth of manner will put you at ease from the start.

He already knows your name, and he won't want to put you to the disadvantage of addressing him as 'Mr Er – er', or compel you to call him 'Sir', which sometimes sounds unnecessarily subservient.

Don't sit down until you

I need to break the ice quickly. Is the candidate mature and reasonably confident, or does he need helping? (Perhaps by extra sympathy of manner, or by sharing a humorous aside with him. There is nothing like a light touch of humour for getting over a sticky patch, either now or later on.)

What is my first impression of this candidate? If it is favourable, I must probe the substance behind the

Some things for you to bear in mind	Some things your interviewer is thinking about

have been offered a chair, but, equally, don't stand shifting from foot to foot as if you want to visit the toilet.

When you sit, if there is a slight delay while the interviewer adjusts his papers, don't fidget or look round the room. Sit alertly and wait until he is already. (This applies also if there is an interruption – for example, a telephone call – while the interview is taking place.)

initial charm.

If it is unfavourable, it is up to me to draw him out. It would be a pity to miss a sound candidate because for some innocent reason he does not interview well.

2. Checking the facts

Don't assume that, because the interviewer is going over the main facts of your application, he has not already read it with attention. He needs to check the facts to make sure he has fully understood them, to fill any gaps, and to add details to any information that seems a bit scanty.

This is your chance to get used to the sound of the interviewer's voice and his way of putting things.

He is setting a standard in the businesslike conduct of

I have already made some private notes on points I wish to pursue with the candidate. I will check with him particularly those facts I want to follow up later.

Often an 'all-comers' application form does not ask all the questions relevant to specific interviewees. I must ask any such questions now, in a relaxed, face-to-face situation, rather than seek answers later by correspondence.

| **Some things for you to bear in mind** | **Some things your interviewer is thinking about** |

the interview, and you should respond accordingly.

Be ready to offer any supplementary information that you think may help. Don't give it in great detail, but don't withhold it if it helps to round off the picture he is getting of you.

Along with the facts go the reasons (e.g. 'Why did you leave your last job?' 'Why did you study these subjects at a school when another group of subjects might have given you a better chance?', etc.) Give them briefly and frankly.

3. Following up

The interviewer may raise some points from the confidential papers he has about you, or from telephone inquiries he has made.

This is the stage where the interviewer will begin to talk less and expect you to talk more. (E.g. inviting you to describe and develop some experience you have referred to: 'Tell me about . . .' 'What happened when . . .')

This is the time to go over any apparent discrepancies there may be between what the candidate wrote in his application and any other information I have about him. Often such discrepancies are easily explained; where they are not, the reasons may come out later in the interview.

Now to get the candidate talking. My attention is no longer divided between the sheaf of documents and the

Some things for you to bear in mind	**Some things your interviewer is thinking about**

candidate. I can now give him my full attention, with only an occasional glance at my notes.

If my notes occupy too much of my attention it will prove that I haven't done my homework properly.

4. Basic questions

Now we are getting more to the point. He is sizing me up. He knows my qualifications and experience; now he is asking himself whether I am the right kind of person for the place, and whether I am easy to get on with.

He won't learn this from brief, one-word answers. I must expand a bit, without throwing my weight about or being garrulous.

The interview is moving along quite well and I think I am making the right kind of impression.

If I can do well under stress – and you can't say that there's no stress about an interview – he'll know that I can cope with quite a bit.

Up to now, the interview has centred on the candidate's application and the supporting material. Now the emphasis must shift to the position he hopes to fill.

I know the kind of person we are looking for, and I am learning quite a lot about the candidate. Soon I shall have to make up my mind whether I can see him successfully coping with what the position demands.

I shall have to tell him all those things that can't really be expressed in an advertisement, but are better told in a relaxed person-to-person way at the actual interview.

I shall be interested in his reaction because it will reveal whether he can see

Some things for you to bear in mind	**Some things your interviewer is thinking about**

himself successfully occupying the position.

If the candidate has any doubts about whether he really wants what he has put in for, now is the time to find out.

5. Further questions in depth

He's going into more detail now. He wouldn't do this if he wasn't interested in me. Now is my chance to show my strength. I think it pays, though, to be frank about any failures or disappointments that may come up. I can balance these by expanding on things that have gone well and my hopes for the future. Perhaps he'll let me lead off from some of his questions to other things that might help me but that he doesn't yet know about.

If the candidate himself has expressed some doubt about whether he really wants to proceed with his application, he need not detain me much longer. Nor need I keep a candidate who has already shown that he is definitely not the kind of person we are looking for.

But the majority of interviewees, who show acceptable qualities, are worth probing further, to see what extra strengths they have to offer. The 'plus' qualities will probably be decisive – unless the field is a very poor one.

Our conversation has already suggested some possibilities worth pursuing now.

I must also find out about anything which might prevent the candidate giving of

Some things for you to bear in mind	Some things your interviewer is thinking about
	his best. (Family tensions? Absorbing outside interests that could be a source of strength, but carried too far may mean weakness?) I have to be tactful here, because I must not go beyond our legitimate concern.

6. An opportunity for the candidate to present further facts or to ask questions

This really is the last chance. If I have nothing else to say, at least I can round off the interview with a comment which compliments the interviewer on covering the ground so thoroughly by his questions that I am satisfied now to leave it to him.	My questioning has set trains of thought going in his mind as well as mine. This is his last chance to round off the picture of himself.
	I can also settle any doubts in answering his questions.
	I shall perhaps be able to gauge his interest and enthusiasm by the sort of question he asks.

7. Rounding it off

I now know how long my period of suspense will be, but I wonder whether I can tell from his manner whether I have been successful?	I must tell him when he can expect to learn the result of the interview.
Anyway, I will leave	I may be able to give him an indication of success; but whether I can or not, I can at least express an interest

Some things for you to bear in mind	Some things your interviewer is thinking about
confidently and on good terms with him. Even if I am unsuccessful this has been a useful and interesting experience.	in him and in what he had to offer. I hope he leaves feeling that he has had a fair hearing.

Don't Let Anything Throw You Off Balance!

It is easy to give advice like this, but, humanly speaking, no one can guarantee himself a cool and relaxed interview in all circumstances. The best we can do is to be aware of things that might put us to disadvantage and perhaps sap our confidence.

An interviewer needs to probe beneath our guard, to discover a real person, with strengths and weaknesses. Strengths are respected and their potentialities assessed; the extent of weaknesses needs to be known, and so does our capacity to remedy them. (Education and training will put right some weaknesses.)

Some weaknesses are personal to ourselves. If you have a tendency to blush, stammer, or show obvious signs of nervousness, you may be sure that a 'stress' situation like an interview is more likely to bring it on than a casual chat about nothing in particular. If you are apt to resent 'prying' into your affairs, you may not like some of the personal questions that are bound to be asked, and your emotional temperature will rise accordingly. If this happens, you will not find it easy to gather or express your thoughts, and you will probably become very self-conscious about the impression you are creating. In an emotionally charged situation like this, you could quite easily misread your interviewer's attitude and intentions towards you. He probably feels more sympathetic than you think.

It doesn't do to be too sensitive. Take the situation as philosophically as you can. Look outward rather than inward. Concentrate on the interviewer as well as his questions. Try him with a smile. Keep your attention on his face (but not so fixedly that you look as if you'd like to murder him). You are the focus of his attention: let him be the focus of yours.

Like most people, you are probably not unduly sensitive, and you can answer up for yourself in a reasonably forthright yet courteous manner. What, then, can go wrong?

Here are some things that may affect you:

The pace of questions may hot up.
The interviewer may be aware of other candidates whom he must see. The programme of interviews may be running late, and he doesn't want delays to get worse.

Or, he may find the interview with you dragging a bit, and force the pace in a way which is a cue to you to get a move on.

Or, he may think you have a tendency to ramble or introduce irrelevancies, so he fires brief questions at you to keep you to the point. (*His* point, remember.)

Or he may want to see how you cope with questions that crowd in on each other. Do you easily get rattled? Can you deal with them at a fast pace? (Being able to respond quickly and adequately to matters that arise suddenly might be vital in the job you are seeking.) If you are rather deliberate in your thought and speech, don't let your interviewer hurry you unduly. He may respect you more for the seriousness with which you take his questions than for the rather trivial, staccato, off-the-cuff answers you may be tempted to give.

Questions may switch suddenly from one topic to another.
This can happen because the main themes of the interview have been covered, and the interviewer wants to settle a number of points to round off his picture of you.

A sudden change of topic catches nearly everyone off guard, so an interviewer may use this method if he suspects that there are matters you wish to avoid, or to cover up.

He may use the method, too, to return to a topic on which he was not really satisfied with your earlier answers.

Your interviewer may make remarks which have an 'edge' to them, and which you may find unfair, so that, in self-defence, you feel compelled to reply to set the record straight.
He might say, for example, 'I am getting the impression that you're willing to do things that you're interested in, but resent being asked to do others, however vital they are'.

Or, bluntly, 'I think you're lazy'.

Perhaps he means to shake you out of complacency with needling remarks, or perhaps he is voicing aloud doubts that he has at the back of his mind.

If this happens to you, try not to feel aggressive, or too much on the defensive. Take the criticism seriously. It is better to know how you appear to an interviewer than to be left in the dark and perhaps give a similarly unfortunate impression at the next interview.

You might begin by saying 'I think I know why I have given you this impression, but . . .' If you can go some way towards agreeing with a criticism before you offer a more favourable explanation, at least you will show that you can recognize a fault in yourself, and perhaps that you are doing something to correct it.

If you refuse to accept a well-meant criticism, your interviewer may think as badly of you for believing 'He's got it all wrong' as you think of him. You don't make a friend of your interviewer in this way.

Any Matters Arising?
When the details on your written applications have been checked, they are almost certain to suggest further questions to your interviewer. The actual questions will depend on the nature of your application, but you will have no difficulty in judging which of the following lines of inquiry could arise in your particular case. The

questions below will probably not be asked as they are given, but they are indications of what is in the interviewer's mind:

Your education

Was your education what might have been expected for one of your ability and background?

Did anything hold you back, or, on the other hand, give you any advantages?

Did you make steady progress during your school (College, University) career?

Did you rise to the opportunities offered by your school (College, University) to gain qualifications?

How do you account for any exam failures you have had, particularly in vital subjects? How do you account for any persistent failure in a subject important to you?

Do you expect success in any exams coming up?

Have you got the right balance of subjects for a person of your particular talents?

Are your subjects so broadly based that they don't really reveal your strengths? Or are they so narrowly specialist that they aren't much use to you unless an employer wants exactly what you offer and no more?

Are there any unexpected gaps in the subjects (or qualifications) you have to offer? If so, what are you doing to remedy them?

What grades are your passes? Couldn't you have done better?

Why didn't you take this subject? Why did you drop that? Why didn't you carry the other to a higher level?

Your work

Changes of job. Why? Why so many (so few) changes? Did all the changes lead to greater experience, more responsibility, promotion?

How long did you stay in your last job? (Or, why do you want to leave your present job?)

Do you enjoy your work? Job-satisfaction: what does this mean to you? What really motivates you?

What do you expect to get from the job for which you are applying, that you don't get from your present job? What have you really got to offer us?

Do you understand what the job for which you are applying entails?

How did you hear of us?

What was the exact nature of the work in your last (present) job?

What degree of responsibility did you hold?

Bear in mind that questions arise from testimonials and references as well as from your written application. This is especially true of the most recent stages of your career, whether in some form of education or at work.

You know what your testimonials say, because you sent in copies with your application yourself, and you must have a fair idea of what your referees have said about you. Now put yourself in the position of your interviewer: could any questions arise from the information or views they have expressed about you?

Some Questions You Should Be Prepared For
When you come up for interview you probably have a fair idea of what you are likely to be asked. You may be surprised, though, at the range of questions fired at you, and you may feel that some of them pry unnecessarily into your private affairs.

How can it be anyone else's concern, you may wonder, how you spend your free time? If you are married, you may feel suspicious if you are asked whether your wife (or husband) supports you in your application. Surely this is your own business, and no one else's?

Now look at it in this way. Would you feel happy if the people for whom you worked regarded you merely as a pair of hands? Or as an able-bodied robot? Or as a set of skills to be used according to demand? You would more likely want to shriek out that you are a person too, with human wants and feelings and rights.

The wider questions asked at interview help to fill out

the picture of you as a person. They help to show whether you are likely to 'fit in', whether you are easy to get on with, whether you possess ambition and are likely to work hard, or be a frequent absentee. They help to show whether you possess the requisite qualities and have the time, the energy, and the will to use them.

Those making appointments are only too well aware of the family, social, and economic pressures that can turn an otherwise satisfactory person into a harassed individual doing slapdash work and exercising a demoralizing influence on others. A good background is therefore reassuring to those making appointments. Can you blame them for not wanting to buy trouble?

In cases like these, frankness is important. There should be no hint of holding back, or concealing what might be a bit damaging.

You might agree about the importance of frankness, but what is the good of frankness if it leads to your application being turned down without an interview at all?

There is a possible compromise here. You might faithfully fill in your application form without drawing attention to an awkward fact, and rely on giving the proper background and interpretation to it in the person-to-person interview situation. In this situation you will at least get a hearing, and almost certainly the chance to establish your sincerity by your speech and bearing. If there is anything to your detriment, it is best to say it yourself and get it over with, rather than have it dragged from you. Say it, and move quickly on to more favourable ground.

Sometimes you have simply got to refer to an awkward fact at the application stage. An example of this is when you lack what is usually regarded as an essential qualification.

If you made no reference to the omission, they might simply think that you hadn't properly read the conditions, and put your application straight into the waste paper basket. In the space where you were expected to enter details of the qualification you could put 'Please see covering letter', or 'Please see general remarks at end'.

The covering letter solution is probably better than trying to fit an explanation into the small space they allow on most forms. See that the letter is firmly clipped or fastened to the form, and don't let yourself be lured into such a lengthy explanation that the letter is unlikely to be read.

A problem for the interviewer is how far he can take the candidate's word on questions about himself. Can he believe him all along the line? Is the candidate a yes-man (for the purpose of the interview) anxious to please and to be well-thought-of? Will his determination to gain acceptance outweigh his honesty?

One way of checking is for the interviewer to ask a good many questions and to see whether a consistent pattern emerges. If it doesn't, the candidate may be confronted at a later stage with a statement he made earlier and asked to explain the difference.

Spontaneous, straightforward answers given without hesitation carry conviction, particularly if they are backed up by a frank, open manner.

When an interviewer suspects that a candidate is 'going along' with him, agreeing a shade too readily with his line of thought and not expressing any doubts or qualifications, he may test the candidate with some statement bordering on the outrageous, and then express surprise that the candidate agreed with it.

This can happen so innocently. Beware of being lured gently on, perhaps with a line of thought you hadn't previously considered. You say 'Yes' almost mechanically, and are then faced with the logic of the position you have taken up.

You need to be cautious (but not irritatingly ultra-cautious) and to think before you answer. If you don't understand a question, ask the interviewer to repeat it, or to put it in a different way. Or you can re-phrase it yourself, asking 'Do you mean . . .?'

Another approach is to think your answer out aloud,

prefacing what you say with the comment that the question has several implications, and going on to give what you think is involved, before attempting a final answer.

No interviewer expects a candidate to be a human slot-machine from which pops an immediate complete answer. If you give a quick response to every question asked, you could be suspected of saying the first thing that comes into your head and sticking to it, right or wrong. Don't be afraid to admit that an answer was a bit hasty, and that on further thought you would put it differently.

Among the subjects which can lead to follow-up questions which might betray you into giving ill-considered judgements are the following:

> Explanations of why your education or career took the time it did.
> Criticisms of teachers, employers, authorities.
> Opinions you express on people, firms, policies.
> Likes and dislikes. Personal preferences.
> 'I see you had an interview for ... You weren't accepted. What went wrong?'

Bear in mind that a question is not always what it seems to be. For example, the interviewer might ask a candidate 'Do you ever lose your temper? (or get excited, shout at anyone, enjoy an argument)' but the question at the back of his mind may be rather different. It could be 'Are you as dull as you seem to be?'

Or, it might be 'You sound a bit opinionated. Are you aggressive with it? Do you rub people up the wrong way?'

Or might it simply be a wish to see another side of the candidate. If he has been fairly forthcoming, yet too smoothly neutral, his interviewer may hope to see the light of enthusiasm (or battle, or protest) in his eyes.

Question and answer are stimulus and response. The right question will provoke an informative answer – and not just in the form of words.

The words have got to be right, of course, but in giving them the candidate reveals much more. He shows:

94

how quickly he appreciates the point of what he is being asked,

how he marshals the facts before he replies,

how he handles an account, an argument, an explanation,

what his priorities are, and what he selects for emphasis,

what he rejects, or dismisses as insignificant,

in gesture (sometimes in place of words, and sometimes in support of them) he may show surprise, annoyance, perplexity, anxiety, fear, hope, enlightenment, etc.

Some candidates use the vocabulary of gesture much more than others. This is particularly so with face and hands but also with shifts of position and direction of glance.

Words can be used to conceal as well as reveal. It is less easy to conceal through gesture. If a candidate made up his mind to prevent his gestures from revealing his private hopes or anxieties he would probably sit stiff and poker-faced, and create the same impression as if he answered every question with a monosyllable or brief phrase. If the interviewer could not draw him out he might be dismissed as one with little to offer.

It is part of an interviewer's job to see that a candidate does not lose by showing a nervousness which is perfectly natural and understandable.

The easiest and most relaxing question you might be asked at interview is the simple one 'You're nervous, aren't you?' and with a nod, a smile, and a deep breath your nervousness has gone.

'What do you read?'

This is one of a number of questions designed to discover a candidate's alertness, his common observation, and his interest in people, things, and ideas.

Variations on this question are:

'Do you read for information?'

Most practical people do. They needn't feel ashamed of missing the classics of literature. Their temperament and talent lead them to facts, know-how, and personal skills. The interviewer will be interested to learn whether their factual reading is up-to-date and links adequately with their aims; whether it is understood and critically received. The practical person can surely be expected to be aware of the magazines, journals, and newspaper columns which cater for his interests. More than this: he can be expected to be taking a close and continuing interest in them.

'Do you read for pleasure?'

This seems a lightweight question, but answers to it sometimes throw considerable light on whether or not the candidate is a well-balanced individual. Is he such a serious-minded specialist that he is blind to the influences that affect other people? If so, how is he going to get on with them in his work? Is he already in a mental rut that he will find it harder and harder to get out of?

You, as a candidate, needn't fear earning a low opinion because you read Wilbur Smith (or whoever else you care to name) rather than Shakespeare. If your reading gives you pleasure, at least the question touches your enthusiasm, and you can be expected to say why you enjoy your favourite author or why you like a certain type of book.

It is a painful experience for an interviewer to see a candidate who reads very little, or nothing at all, dredging up from his memory the title of a book read long ago. If you can't do better than say 'Black Beauty' (an answer I have heard to this question) it is best to shut up.

'What newspaper do you read?'

It doesn't matter what newspaper you name. It is the follow-up that concerns your interviewer. What do you look for in the paper, and what do you think you get out of it?

This is a question which sometimes leads to a good deal of verbal sparring without much information. The interviewer wants to know what catches your eye and makes you read further. He wants to know what you positively seek out in the paper. He might ask what you read first, and then next.

It's no use claiming to read 'everything'. Your interviewer will raise his eyebrows and probably repeat the word. 'Everything?' And then you will have to climb down and say what you do read.

It's not very informative, either, to claim that you read the headlines. You probably do. He is more interested in the kind of headline that encourages you to read on.

In getting you to talk about the newspaper, your interviewer won't want to feel that he's putting ideas into your head. If you are vague about your reading, he won't want to have to ask you whether you prefer home news to foreign, or sport to both of them. He won't want to name the various sections of the paper so that you can say 'Yes' to the one that sounds most promising. He'll end by suspecting, perhaps rightly, that you don't read the papers at all, except to see the headlines you couldn't possibly miss, the sports results you are interested in, and the big advertisement spreads.

A wider form of question is: *'From what source do you get most of your knowledge of the world around you?'*
It might be from the newspaper, from TV, from radio, or from discussions with your friends.

You should be prepared to follow up a question like this in whatever direction your interviewer takes it:

Writers, programmes, personalities you have come to rely on (or admire, or despise, etc.). What is there about them that inspires your interest (admiration, contempt, etc.)?

Are you a random viewer (listener, reader), switching off if a programme is not to your liking, or do you positively look out for particular programmes (people, topics)?

Do you discuss world (local, political) affairs with your friends?

Be prepared for a ruthlessly factual question or two:

'What's in the papers today?'

'What important event is taking place in . . .?'

'What is your opinion on the controversy about . . .?

'How do you use your spare time?'
A wide range of interests suggests a lively mind and an active person. It also suggests a body of experience and personal resource that can be drawn on.

It might, though, point to a nervously active person who attempts a lot of things and drops them at the first sign of difficulty.

Your interviewer will probably try to find out how long and successfully your interests have been pursued, and whether you still keep them up. It's not a good thing to claim, as a piece of window-dressing, that you are interested in a hobby or sport, and then have your interviewer discover that in fact you dropped it years ago. It doesn't matter dropping a pursuit: your interviewer understands as well as you do the pressures on an individual in a busy world.

Questioning you about your spare time will soon tell an interviewer whether you are easily bored or whether you live a full and satisfying life. 'There's nothing to do' tells more about the speaker than about his opportunities. Bored people who live empty lives are more likely to be unhappy and a source of unhappiness in others than people who live busy and varied lives. An interviewer is bound to be concerned with the effect a candidate has on future colleagues.

There is another thing your interviewer will be concerned with. Is your life so full, and are you subject to such pressure, that you won't be able to cope with the work properly if he accepts you? (If you fear giving this impression, you could say what you would drop if you find you've taken on too much.)

Questions concerning spare time can cover such wide ground that they can quite easily touch sensitive spots. Suppose you are an active political worker, or a keen supporter of a particular church, or have family (or boy-friend or girl-friend) troubles – are you expected to be forthcoming about these too? Would it pay (or tell against you) to identify yourself with a political party, or a church that might not have your interviewer's approval?

Discussion is more free and open these days than it used to be, and it is easy to exaggerate the fear that your private beliefs will be frowned on. (Come to that, your interviewer might share them.)

In sensitive areas it is best to proceed with caution but not concealment. You can mention political activities or church activities or family matters and leave it to your interviewer to pursue things further if he wants to. After all, it is better to show an active concern for political or religious or social affairs than to appear to be the kind of person who leaves all these important things to others.

On a severely practical level, don't become aggressive or defensive or long-winded about sensitive subjects that come up. Let them simply take their limited place in the interview.

'Do you have any cultural interests?'
'Culture' means different things to different people. In an interview context you can take it to mean, simply, 'way of life'. Questions on cultural interests have little or no direct connection with the purpose of your application, or with your interviewer's eventual acceptance or rejection of you.

They are justified because your interviewer is looking at you as a whole person, and not as a pair of hands, a set of skills, or a body of knowledge. Your person-to-person relationships are likely to be all the better if you have wide cultural interests.

(The importance of wide interests is well recognised nowadays. It is the reason, for example, for including liberal studies – under this or some other name – in

College courses, and for the provision of sports and recreational facilities for workpeople.)

An interviewer may not spend much time in questioning you about sport, going to the theatre or cinema, or about TV programmes, but you should not regard it as an intrusion if he does ask a few questions. The same applies to questions on travel here or abroad, holidays you have had, visits you have made, bodies you belong to, people you have met, classes you have attended, and all the miscellaneous things that have interested you.

He is likely to react more favourably where you are an active participant rather than a casual, fairly passive, observer.

'What are your ambitions?'
Or, 'What's your long-term view of this application of yours?'

Have you just applied hopefully, so that if you are accepted you will heave a sigh of relief, flop down in a chair, and say 'I'm there!' Or have you taken a long view of your career, and see your present application as a stage in the planned development and use of your abilities?

It makes a difference! You may be successful with a hopeful and lucky application, but you may drift off again with a similar application elsewhere. But the more you have thought about your career, and planned it in general terms as well as you are able, the more you are likely to gain (and to give) if your application is successful. Your work and progress will be purposive, and you will not be so likely to give up at the first difficulty.

From the interviewer's point of view, it is important that the work should be at your level. He will want to make up his mind whether you are such an able person that you are likely to be dissatisfied with the work, and therefore want to move off at the earliest opportunity (or become a thorn in the flesh). Or whether you will perhaps not be up to the work, and get fed up with it and your lack of progress, with unfortunate consequences for all concerned.

How long you are likely to stay is a critical question. If you're not going to stay long, is it worth saying 'Yes' to your application when they will shortly be looking for someone else to replace you?

Your interviewer needs to be sure that you know what work would be involved if he accepted you. He can bring this out through his questions. To reinforce the answers you give him he may also ask 'How did you get to know of us?' 'Who have you talked to about your application?' 'Where did you get advice from?' 'Have you studied the information we sent with the application form?'

He may even ask 'What do you know about our work?'

You will be able to deduce some questions he will actually ask you from the questions he is bound to ask himself about you:

Has he set his sights too high (too low)?

Will he be a round peg in a square hole?

Is he really committed to us (our work, etc.) or is his application a second-choice one because he couldn't get his first choice? If it is a second-choice (because his first choice was not available, or because he applied for it and was turned down) has he become reconciled to it? Has he really thought about what his choice involves?

Is he cut out for some of the things we do, but not for others? If so, does he expect us to keep him at the things he knows and likes best, so that he can avoid the rest? Doesn't he realise that he must take the rough with the smooth, and accept some unwelcome duties with a good heart?

Ambitions are revealing because they show some degree of self-assessment.

Some ambitions form part of an individual's fantasy-world, and are hopelessly unrealistic. Applications based on fantasy are a try-on. Most people have a sufficiently realistic assessment of their own abilities and interests not to waste their own and others' time on fruitless applications, but some are so blinkered that they don't realise their limitations.

'After all, if you don't bung in an application, you'll never know your luck, will you?' is the attitude they take. Most unrealistic applications are sifted out at the application stage; very few lead to a call-up for interview. But all interviewers face, at one time or another, the odd candidate who causes the interviewer to wonder, in the course of the conversation, how on earth he came to be called up at all. An interview like this is likely to be brief, polite, and conclusive.

(An interviewer is probably used to telling candidates that they will be told the result of the interview by letter in a week or so, and he may adopt this method with the odd unsatisfactory candidate under discussion. He could express his regret and explain why the application must fail, but he is more likely to spare himself a wrangle by sticking to the usual formula. This is a pity in one way, because the candidate may put in an equally hopeless application elsewhere, and feel that, when he fails again, he didn't stand a chance. If he lowered his sights he wouldn't lay himself so wide open to disappointment.)

Don't be afraid to reveal your hopes and ambitions. Your own thought about them beforehand rules out all but the tiniest possibility that they contain an element of fantasy. Expressing reasonable (and even rather hopeful) ambitions may well reinforce the view your interviewer already holds of you as a person with something about him. After all, ambition argues a willingness to work hard in order to achieve it.

'What do you think you have to offer us?'
This is a difficult question, however it is phrased. It might be expressed, a little more delicately, in this way: 'What qualities, do you think, are needed by . . . (the position you are applying for)?'

You answer this, of course, in a considered and

detached way, but as your list lengthens you begin to suspect that you already know the follow-up question. You are probably right. It is: 'Do you think you possess these qualities?'

Putting the question in two parts, like this, is a good deal kinder and less embarrassing than asking it in its bluntest form. But even the blunt question can be put more devastatingly: 'What makes you think that you would make a good . . .?'

Whichever way it comes, be prepared for a fairly downright question on your own assessment of what you have to give – and what it takes. Your interviewer may ease it for you by inviting you not to be too modest.

The question repays careful preparation. You would be lucky if you could draw out of thin air an answer which would withstand a probing follow-up. Yet you don't want to reel off an answer so pat that you have obviously learnt it up.

Self-assessment by a candidate is very revealing from the interviewer's point of view. The candidate is really doing two things. He is selecting the qualities he believes are called for and, by implication, putting them into an order of importance. He is also setting out the qualities he believes he possesses and matching them with the first list. He is both auctioneer and bidder.

Whether the question takes you by surprise, or whether you have thought about it beforehand, don't be afraid to take your time. If you blurt out the first thing that comes into your head you will only be written down as a person who speaks before he thinks.

Pay your interviewer the compliment of taking a difficult question seriously. He will be watching your reaction very closely.

Such a question ought not to take you by surprise. After all, you did put it in an application. You must have considered your prospects and your chances.

You can get your ideas moving with a very brief reiteration of the qualifications, personal skills and experience you set down in your written application. You might then refer to the following matters, in whatever order you think best;

> Getting on with people (a *must* in every job)
> Acceptance of responsibility
> Ability to give and take orders
> Understanding what the firm (undertaking, public body, College, to which you have applied) stands for
> Interests or ideas you would like to pursue if accepted
> Personal qualities: loyalty, co-operativeness, initiative, etc.

Take your time – but try not to ramble on. Leave it to your interviewer to ask you to enlarge on any matter, or to bring your answer to a conclusion. He will stop you when he has heard enough.

Hypothetical questions
The interview may create an imaginary (or real) situation and ask you how you would deal with it – the 'what if . . .' question.

Reply to these questions with care. The situation described may be very similar to a real one which happened recently, and a detailed answer from you may be wrong because you only have a brief description of the position. Answer by explaining the general principles you would apply to such a problem, and perhaps say what you have done in the past in similar circumstances.

11

Have I The Personality For The Job?

One basic question that your interviewer will have to make up his mind about is 'Has he the right personality for the job?'

He will have a preliminary answer or two before he ever sees you. These will come from testimonials and references, from any follow-up telephone calls he might make, and to a limited extent from your own application. He must fill in the rest of the picture from his meeting with you.

Sometimes it is not so much a question of filling in gaps at interview as of revising what he thought he knew about you.

The picture one forms from a written description, no matter how honestly done, is often very different from the reality. An interviewer may, on very rare occasions, have to look through his papers to make sure that they are indeed about the candidate in front of him.

The picture that emerges from interview is developed along the lines of what the interviewer wishes to learn. It can be as detailed and accurate as his skill allows. But the picture from the documents depends on what the writers wished to tell. It may be as helpful or misleading as an Identikit picture. It fails, as all verbal descriptions do, when words mean different things to different people. It fails, sometimes, because the writer of the description does not always have the intimate, up-to-date knowledge of the candidate that the interviewer assumes he has. (A question on the reference form may help to settle this. 'How well do you know the candidate?' 'Very well/fairly well/slightly' gives useful information, especially when coupled with the question 'How long have you known the candidate?')

It may fail, on a small but unknown number of occasions, because a reference is not quite the honest description it purports to be.

The interviewer himself must not fail. The crucial 'Yes' or 'No' depends on his assessment.

He must therefore use some tried and reliable method of assessing all those qualities which can be lumped together under the heading of Personality.

Hunches won't do. The candidate would be at a gross disadvantage if his interviewer thought 'I wouldn't trust him round the corner' as soon as he clapped eyes on him. Or an unfair advantage if the interviewer was beguiled by blue eyes, a ready smile, and an open countenance into thinking that he was just the man for the job.

It wouldn't do, either, if he thought that a candidate couldn't possibly be any good if his eyes were too close together, or if he had a 'lean and hungry look'.

You can't pick interview winners any more than you can pick criminal types on simple rules of thumb like these.

Written personality tests are nowhere near as useful in practice as one might think they should be. At best, they can supplement an interview, and alert an interviewer to a candidate's potential in certain areas – exceptional promise, for example, or weakness likely to lead to failure.

Yet we can take our cue from what such tests attempt. Basically, a personality test is a test of attitudes. If you knew the attitude a person adopts on a sufficiently wide and representative range of issues, you would know all you would need to know about his personality.

The interviewer tries to find out how the candidate looks at life, particularly in those areas that have some bearing on the job for which a decision about him must be made.

Your interviewer already knows what your qualifications are. He knows the levels of your achievement, and (assuming that you did yourself justice on your application form) what further qualifications you hope for. He should also know (making the same assumption) of your membership of any bodies, particularly professional, semi-professional, or 'learned', whose membership implies an important degree of recognition.

Now he wants to look at the person behind the qualifications: the real *you*. What kind of person are you?

There are four basic questions he can ask. They are set out below. Bear in mind that he already has part-answers to these questions. When his answers are complete, he will know enough about you to tell whether he wants you or not.

It is a good plan to look yourself over as if you were your own interviewer. Be as searching as you can about the evidence you produce in support of what you say about yourself. But before you size yourself up, here are the basic questions, with brief notes on what they imply:

(i) *What abilities and aptitudes do you possess?*
Some of your potential will be realized, in the form of intellectual achievements and practical skills; some will not yet be fully developed. Combinations of 'hand and brain'. Interests and aptitudes go strikingly together, so questions about interests may give useful clues about your aptitudes.

(ii) *How well do you get on with others?*
Immediate impression; appearance, grooming, speech, manner: 'impact'; the experience of people who have formed your acquaintance, of your friends, of those who depend on you, look up to you, take orders from you, etc. Your own view of your relationships.

(iii) *What motivates you?*
Aims you set yourself; steps taken to achieve these aims; how you cope with obstacles.

(iv) *How do you react to your environment?*
Fitting in among people, and in an organization; stability in situations of change, tension, etc.

Size Yourself Up

This isn't a game, nor even a quiz. There can't be a score, because although some qualities (character-traits, attitudes, etc.) are necessary in every human setting, others only become important according to the needs of a particular job. Often, it is a combination of qualities that matters, not those qualities in isolation. You don't look for leadership, for example, in those on the bottom rung of the ladder (though followership has its qualities too). You wouldn't be very impressed by a middle-rung aspirant who can give orders and see that they are carried out, but doesn't readily take orders himself.

To some of the questions below there are no 'right' answers. When you try to answer them you will see why. (The first half-dozen questions are cases in point. There are others dotted about, too.) The answer that the inter-viewer is after will come, in these cases, either from his interpretation of what you 'really' mean, or from your answer to a follow-up question.

Are you happy in your work?
You may be happy because you are in a rut, or because you find work challenging and stimulating.

You may be unhappy because the work is tiresome and undemanding, or it is more than you can reasonably cope with.

Are you always on the go?
You may be a hard worker, but you could be working yourself to death and causing tension in those around

you; your own hard work may lead you to expect too much of others.

You may find it hard to relax because you think that relaxing proves that you are losing your grip.

Can you bear anyone to disagree with you?
You may be on the defensive, a bit unsure of yourself. You may be over-confident, and find it hard to accept that you might possibly be wrong.

Do you take too much on?
You may be a willing horse, or you may lack the courage to say 'No'.

You may enjoy tackling a tough assignment, or you may not realize your limitations.

Does success go to your head?
You may be capable of doing better, but decide to rest on your reputation.

You may be unable to accept failure, and so set yourself unrealistic targets.

Do you 'pass the buck'?
You may say 'It isn't my job' to relieve yourself of responsibility.

Or you may hang on to jobs because you can't bear to see others bungle them.

Aggression
Do you ever lose your temper?

When did you last feel 'I've heard enough of their arguments. I must put them right'?

Do you ever lay down the law to your friends?

What do you do if you can't get your way?

What would you be prepared to do to achieve some aim that is important to you?

Getting on with people
Are you a good mixer?

In the give-and-take of everyday life, do you think you matter as much as most people you mix with?

Do people notice you?

Do they respect your opinions?

Do you think that people trust you?

If you had a good idea, and put it forward to a group of your friends, how would it go down?

If an important decision was to be made by a body you belong to, would other members ask your opinion?

Are you a good 'committee man'?

Can you catch other people's eyes easily?

Would they bother to catch yours?

Do people agree with your point of view more often than not?

Do you have opinions, but keep quiet about them?

Have you many friends?

Are you a nervous person?

Do you 'go with the crowd'?

Do you ever 'go it alone'?

Can you enthuse other people?

Do you enjoy meeting the public (or new people)?

Do you possess leadership qualities?

Do you find it difficult to make your mind up?

Do you often change your mind?

Can you give orders (or express a point of view, or make an explanation) briefly and clearly?

Do people understand what you say to them?

Do they argue the point?

Can you get people to work quickly and willingly for you?

Are you able to demonstrate what you want others to do?

Could you yourself do what you demand of others?

Do you have to assert yourself to make your presence felt?

Are you an official of any body you belong to?

Can you give an example or two of leadership you have exercised in a setting similar to that in the job for which you are applying?

A mixed bag of questions (do you think any of them unfair?)
Are you an extrovert or an introvert (or a bit of both)?

Would you call yourself observant?

What have you done lately that you are proud of?

Are there any faults that you think you possess?

Can you take responsibility?

Are you good at handling money?

Can you admit to making a mistake? And retrieve the situation gracefully and effectively?

Have you ever cheated?

Do you possess initiative?

Can you work without supervision?

Do you need a lot of encouragement?

Do you give up easily?

Do you need watching?

Are you apt to waste time?

Are you well-balanced?

Can you grasp ideas (methods, what a situation needs) quickly?

Have you the personal resource to cope with . . . (a problem related to your job)?

Are you rather an emotional person?

Are you a difficult person to work with?

Do you rub people up the wrong way?

Are you trustworthy?

Are you a person of principle? What happens when your principles are hard to achieve?

Can you achieve effective working compromises with people in order to get things done?

How do you react in situations of strain?

Are you a 'character'?

Can you learn from experience?

Are you a good organizer?

Are you a good judge of people?

Could you offer evidence to back up your answers?

(Did you think any of the questions unfair?
If so, there's nothing you can do about it!)

12

Other Issues

Do You Belong to a Special Category?
Most applicants for a post, or a place in College or
University, offer pretty well what is expected of them. In
any large bunch of applicants, however, there are bound
to be a few who do not fall into the normal category. This
can happen for quite innocent reasons, and is not always
to the disadvantage of the applicant.

Special applicants usually need special consideration, and questions to such applicants (and inquiries
made about them too) are likely to be exceptionally
probing.

Among candidates in a special category are the following. Are you, for example:

One who is rather older (or rather younger) than most
recruits to the job.

The interviewer may wonder whether you are older
and therefore insufficiently adaptable, or younger and
insufficiently experienced.

One with fewer than the asked-for qualifications.

Why apply, then? Is some quality or experience
offered which is a good substitute for the missing qualification? Is this just a try-on, in the hope that the field is
so small that personality rather than qualifications will
get the job?

One who has stayed too long in one job (or has drifted from job to job).

> The right sort of person? Too set in someone else's ways? Will re-training be a problem? Is the candidate's heart really in this application?

One who was dismissed from his previous place (or has had applications elsewhere rejected, or is rather hopelessly putting applications in here, there, and everywhere).

> Can we afford other people's rejects? Is he worth interviewing at all?

One with theoretical knowledge but no practical experience (or vice versa).

> Has he had the chance to make up the deficiency but passed the opportunity by? Does he expect us to fill the gap for him?

A woman applying for a job usually done by a man (or vice versa).

> This is less of a hindrance than it used to be. Employers are becoming much more open-minded and anyway we are not supposed to be discriminate. It could be an interesting and worthwhile possibility.

One who has come from abroad with qualifications (or experience, or both) which are not quite relevant here.

> Is he worth the risk? Would he fit in?

One who is 'changing course' and making almost a new career for himself.

> Why?

One with an unfortunate record: a handicap, long unemployment (or marking time in some inappropriate occupation), ill-health, an ex-prisoner, etc.

> Despite the record, is he a worth-while risk? Can we help him? Can he help us?

A woman who is seeking work (or to continue her earlier kind of work) after bringing up a family.

> Is she a poor prospect set against better qualified youngsters? Or is her greater maturity and experience a positive asset?

Another example, which is normal and certainly not a

special category except in an extreme case, is worth including here because it too, may need special probing questions:

One who has come from a different firm (or public authority, etc.) with different ways of doing things.

Is he adaptable? Is his experience going to be an asset, or will he feel – and let us know he feels – that his former way of doing things is right, and ours is wrong?

Can You Get By On Charm?

A lot of people think you can. They believe that honest merit is often overlooked in favour of pleasing and rather superficial manners. These manners, they think, are a gift of nature to some lucky people, who have discovered that they can succeed with them while others, more hardworking and talented than the charmers, are overlooked.

What is charm? Dictionaries aren't much help. It is a quality that is almost indefinable, but we can easily recognize those who are fortunate enough to possess it. It includes ease of manner, assurance, smoothness in dealing with people – and these are all 'pluses'.

It wouldn't do to assume that those who possess these polished, engaging qualities have little else to offer. If the interviewer can't separate the superficial from what has some depth to it, then he is not up to his job.

Some people are extroverts and some are introverts. The former are the sociable ones. This category includes the show-offs, the life-and-soul-of-the-party types, and all those who shine in company. Public figures are nearly all extroverts.

Introverts include those who prefer their own company, 'shrinking violets', 'social isolates', 'bookish' people, and those who do not need much company to pursue their interests and get on.

The out-and-out extrovert would be an embarrassingly tiresome person, claiming everyone's attention and feeling wretched if he were not at the centre of affairs.

The out-and-out introvert, going his own way and

positively shunning company, would be eccentric and almost impossible to get on with.

We are all a bit of a mixture, but most of us incline more to the one than the other. The charmer, by his nature, inclines to extroversion, and if an interviewer accepted his charms too readily he would be overlooking the quieter qualities of those less ready to display themselves.

There can be no doubt, though, that the interview situation is more ready-made for the extrovert than the introvert. The introvert would be asking for trouble if he left it entirely to his interviewer to discover his qualities. An interview is a partnership, and even the introvert must put what he offers on show.

Prejudice In The Interview

Are interviews ever decided on 'hunches'? Does an interviewer turn one candidate down, thinking 'There's something about him I don't like', or accept another with the thought 'I took to him at once'?

Of course an interview can be decided on a hunch. It would be unrealistic to deny this. Every interviewer, like all other human beings, has his prejudices, and he cannot leave them outside the room where he sits in his formal capacity. But at least he can be aware that he is as liable to be prejudiced as the next man, and try to allow for this.

He can standardize his questions and his methods sufficiently to gather comparable information from all those he interviews, so that he doesn't, through prejudice, omit some questions which might have thrown a different, and better, light on an interviewee who doesn't create an immediately favourable impression. He must be flexible too, and ask follow-up questions which develop out of answers to earlier ones.

One common-sense safeguard against prejudice on the part of an individual interviewer is to have a second interviewer, or a panel of interviewers. It is possible, of course, for a whole panel to be prejudiced: they may get on well together and value each other's judgement simply because they have a common background of experience, of education, and of prejudice.

If we tried to devise a method of interviewing which came near to ironing out prejudice, we should almost certainly find that it was so standardized, objective, soulless, and inhuman that its operation would produce worse results than the system it sought to cure.

One form of prejudice is the 'Old Boy network' or the influence of the 'Old School tie'. This is probably much rarer than is generally supposed but can be used as an excuse by disgruntled candidates who can claim (in their own minds) that their failure was due to no fault of their own but to 'privileges' enjoyed by another. But where it is thought to operate, there is nothing the candidate can do about it – except to the extent that it may put him on his mettle.

If he goes into the interview already disgruntled, he is likely to come out dissatisfied. If he goes in in a more positive frame of mind, it is at least on the cards that his interviewer will think twice about rejecting him.

More insidious than this form of prejudice is the so-called 'halo effect'. This happens when interviewer and candidate hit it off because they discover that they have important interests (values, experiences, etc.) in common.

The candidate, having acquired a halo for certain things to his credit, is looked at especially favourably for other things too.

An interviewer has to repress himself to some extent. It would be quite improper for him to steal the limelight. He may need to repress himself still more if he finds himself warming to a candidate simply because of shared interests that may have precious little to do with the job.

Promises, Promises

Situations sometimes arise when a candidate (and sometimes an interviewer) thinks back to the interview and wonders what exactly *was* said.

An interviewer would be inexperienced or careless if he did not take proper on-the-spot notes, however brief, of this highly important transaction. Notes are kept 'for the record'; they are available if queries arise, or to pass on to colleagues who have an interest in appointments. They provide useful information when decisions are made about minimum qualifications and other basic matters. Records, as a whole, show how the type of candidate coming forward changes in the course of years. Interview notes are extremely helpful if the selected candidate decides, after all, not to take up the appointment. There is no need to hold another round of interviews; his notes jog the interviewer's memory when he looks for the 'second string'.

The candidate has no such notes to refresh his memory. If he wonders later what promotion prospects were held out to him, how is he to dredge the facts up from a confused memory of so much said in such a short space of time?

Alternatively, he may have come away with a very clear idea of promises made to him, but when they are not fulfilled he has no way of checking whether the words he thought he heard bear the construction he is so anxious to place upon them. Disappointments and allegations of bad faith can easily stem from the lack of a written record. Difficulties can arise about pay, conditions, prospects, duties, the use of a car, the work-location, or a number of other things.

Knowing that difficulties can arise should alert a candidate to take extra care during the interview itself. When critical areas of work and conditions are under discussion, the candidate can help himself by repeating his interviewer's words. 'Now, have I got this right . . .?' By repeating it to the interviewer for confirmation the candidate is more likely to remember it accurately later. Moreover, he lays himself open to immediate correction if he does happen to have got it wrong.

The most difficult areas arise on the question of prospects. An employer may be recruiting a person who, if all goes well, could in a few years' time step into the shoes of a retiring Director of Partner.

But there are bound to be provisos. Obviously the

applicant must work well and show the right aptitudes during the intervening period. Or the promotion itself could be less than definite since it might only be given if won against competition from others in the same firm. Or it could be subject to the approval of some large shareholder who might have other ideas and a lot of influence.

It is in circumstances of this kind that the applicant should be absolutely clear as to what he and the interviewer have agreed, and should ask for it to be confirmed in writing, perhaps in a formal letter of appointment. This is particularly important if the promises refer, rather vaguely, to some time in the future, or when they hinge on decisions or policies yet to be finalized. It is precisely in these circumstances, of course, that the interviewer needs to guard himself, so that he cannot be as definite as he would like to be. Many promises must therefore remain at the verbal level.

If promises are made verbally, and are not likely to be referred to in a letter of appointment, it would be well for the candidate to jot them down for his own record, while they are still fresh in his memory, ready to be produced or referred to if ever this becomes necessary.

A candidate may make his share of promises too. He may express his willingness to move house, if necessary, or to follow some course to improve his qualifications, or to be available for duties outside normal hours, etc. He must not be surprised if his employer is as anxious to keep him up to the mark as the other way about.

Definite promises made on both sides should be included in the Contract of Employment, a formal document which by law must be given to the employee within 13 weeks of commencement. It lays down the terms and conditions of employment.

Why Do Some Candidates Succeed . . . And Others Fail?
It is a happy situation when an interviewer realises that, when introductions are over and the candidate is sitting comfortably, there is no need for a warm-up conversation, but the interview can go forward to business straight

away. It is a compliment to the candidate too, that he has made an immediate impact. His presence, bearing, maturity, responsiveness, and forthcoming manner have all declared themselves, and he gains as well from the relaxed yet workmanlike atmosphere.

Does it surprise you that an interview can be a pleasure? It shouldn't. When an interview drags, it is because a candidate (or the interviewer!) is reserved, uncertain, ultra-cautious, or plain dull, and the process of breaking down the barriers can be time-consuming and sometimes rather wearing.

It is a welcome surprise when a candidate shows at once that no such process is necessary. In this case, the candidate gains as much as the interviewer does, and the pleasure is reciprocal.

Usually, an interview confirms the impression gained from the written application, but sometimes the face-to-face encounter produces a different impression. This may be because the active personal presence is more positive than a painstakingly written document. Or perhaps, on the other hand, because a candidate finds it easier to be forthcoming on paper than his shyness or inadequacy allows him to be in person.

Undeniably, there is an element of luck in being successful in landing a job (less so, perhaps, in keeping it). A successful application depends on a coincidence: a candidate's knowledge, skill, and personality match reasonably well the job that is going at the time the candidate is free to offer himself.

There is sometimes an element of hard luck when a candidate fails. (But not so often as candidates would have you believe.)

Questions of luck apart, there are some reasons for failure that are well worth considering. The following are some of them:

1. *Qualifications do not match requirements.*
   If the difference between qualifications and requirements is too great, the applicant won't be called for

interview at all. He has merely aimed at the wrong target.

If the difference is slender, the applicant may be called for interview for one of several reasons: there may be a poor field; or the candidate may be worth seeing because he might possess other qualities or experience to counterbalance the discrepancy; or the discrepancy might be fairly easily remedied by training; or there might be special circumstances of a 'hard luck' nature which make it worthwhile to see him.

2. *Personal qualities do not match requirements.*
The applicant may be immature, or so apparently young for his age that his colleagues, contacts, customers, etc., might not take him sufficiently seriously. He might be dull, unobservant, unresponsive, lacking in ambition and drive. Perhaps experience at school (and later) did not stimulate him sufficiently: perhaps the stimulus was there but he did not accept the challenge.

3. *The candidate creates conditions of failure for himself by not studying the market.*
If he is a candidate for a place at College or University, he may not have informed himself about the subjects pre-requisite for the courses he wants to take. If he is an applicant for a job in commerce or industry, and has misjudged the market, he may have over-valued what he has to offer. Is he an incurable optimist? Has panic led him to apply on too wide a front?

Or it may become clear that the applicant has not made any study at all of the Company he is applying to, and knows nothing of its products, its advertisements, or its subsidiaries and their activities. Candidates for top-level appointments need to demonstrate a shrewd assessment of profits/losses and balance sheets, and need to have followed the recent progress and development of the Company sufficiently well to say what it is that they like about it.

4. *The candidate's experience may be inadequate, or of the wrong sort.*
   Too many changes of job? Is he a drifter? Why does he think he can make a success of a job with us? Is he flying a kite? Can we wholly trust his description of his previous job successes, or of his reason for leaving earlier jobs? Is he more of a talker than a doer? He is evidently willing to take the risk of switching jobs or taking on something new, but can we afford to take the risk with him?

After some interviews, the interviewer is expected to note down the reasons for failure (perhaps for colleagues, or to pass on to another body interviewing the candidate). What kind of reasons are given?

An out-and-out failure (such as 'He will never make a . . .') is rarely recorded. Nearly always there is something to be said on the positive side. A candidate may be personable, yet unaware of what he would be taking on if he were accepted. He may have developed extremely well a narrow range of talents, and yet show little or no promise in other fields just as vital. He may think his strengths will get him through, and be unaware of the extent of his weaknesses.

'Failures' at interview can never be eliminated, but the number of 'failures' can be reduced by candidates who are prepared to look after their own interests more than some of them do at present. They need to be more realistic and less happy-go-lucky in their applications; they need to study the market more; they need to appraise their own skills and knowledge more carefully (and, often, bring them up-to-date); they need to plan ahead so that gaining qualifications and experience is part of the job-hunting process.

There is so much in job-hunting (and in place-hunting in Colleges and Universities) that a candidate can do for himself that it is surely fruitless to spend time and energy blaming bad luck or the machinations of those who get there before we do for our lack of success. Those who make appointments are bound to be a bit suspicious of candidates with too many excuses, or who are apt to blame anyone but themselves.

13

Things To Do . . .

Dress the part; act the part.
You owe it to yourself to show that you appreciate what will be expected of you if your application is accepted. Is this 'putting on an act'? Not really. If you can't look as you should do in the interview, is it likely that you will do so when working? You don't want to leave your interviewer wondering whether you are casual and don't care, or whether you are simply unaware of what your application implies.

Be yourself.
Obviously. But you are more than one 'self', aren't you? Or, at least, there are different sides to yourself, and you might as well show the most favourable one. An interview is a matching process. You have to show that you fit the vacancy, the place at College, or wherever the interview leads. You have to do this without giving a false, or strained, impression, and this can only happen if the interviewer sees the real 'you'. If he suspects a façade, he will try to dismantle it. You have been warned!

Show some enthusiasm.
This is clearly a necessity, yet some candidates – perhaps because they are overawed by a sense of occasion – sit stodgily there and don't do any sort of justice to themselves. After all, you *did* apply, and this argues some keenness. Now keep it up.

Things To Avoid . . .

Don't appear sour or disgruntled, or behave as if you bear a grudge or have an axe to grind.
Try to be confident and at least mildly optimistic. Some candidates give an unfortunate impression with lengthy explanations of why they were right and someone else wrong – perhaps in a former job. This looks too much like defensive self-justification. Keep yourself in check if you think you are liable to blame other people, argue with your interviewer, or press a point of view too strongly.

Don't appear over-confident, or boastful.
Exaggerated claims invite doubt, and perhaps incredulity. They lead to searching follow-up questions, and an uncomfortable feeling of deflation for you. One of the worst things you can do is to give the impression that you know your interviewer's business better than he does.

If . . .

If you were accepted . . .
Don't let your new-won confidence on acceptance go to
your head. You still have to make a start at the job itself.
If you made any promises at interview, or expressed hopes
for the future, don't be surprised to be taken at your word.

Success on this occasion should encourage you to try
further in due course.

If you were rejected . . .
What did you learn from the encounter?
Were you surprised by the decision?
Was there an element of bad luck?
Was there a stage when you felt things begin to go wrong?
Did you hit it off with the interviewer?
Did you sense any sort of barrier between you and the
interviewer?
Is there anything you could do about poor communication?
Did any questions take you by surprise?

It's no use blaming the interviewer for failure. He may
have been inexperienced, biased, careless (and whatever
other derogatory adjectives you care to add) but with all
his limitations, he is a fact for you to reckon with. (If he is
as bad as you might think, his employers and associates
will suffer from his poor decisions.) At least you have

experienced a useful and crucial exercise in human relations.

Don't let one unfortunate experience deter you from offering your services elsewhere. At the same time, don't forget that your recent interviewer has his view of the situation. Perhaps he is not as bad – or as good – as you think. If you are prepared to be self-critical you might offer a more streamlined version of yourself to the next interviewer.

Honestly, were you adequately prepared? If not, you can help yourself to better 'luck' next time.

Whatever you do, don't lose heart.

Part 3

Here we deal with the most important element of all,
the CV (or Résumé).

14

Your CV:
The Basics

The challenges of the twenty-first century are going to prove more exciting for some than for others. Technological progress will continue to offer great opportunities and an improved life style to those in the forefront. Others will find a steadily declining demand for their services, as computer brains encroach further into the workplace. Permanently high levels of unemployment throughout the civilised world are turning job applicants into competitors for a prize: the prize being the job at the end of it all. This is where the CV comes into focus.

I use the term CV (Curriculum Vitae) throughout, because this is the common expression in Great Britain. But in the USA and many other parts of the world where this book is read, the term 'Résumé' is more common. The two are interchangeable, mean exactly the same, and this is just an example of the rich diversity of development that the English language displays in different parts of the globe. But to save needless repetitions of the alternative, I mostly use the term CV in the rest of this book.

While many people have a vague idea of how to put a CV together, those who have gone thoroughly into the whys and wherefores beforehand are much more likely to be invited to an interview. A rather unfortunate pitfall awaiting applicants who are making a genuine, all-out effort is the poor quality of advice bandied about by so-called 'experts'. This can lead applicants to undersell themselves disastrously, by causing them to offer too little information.

The purpose of Part 3 is to provide an easy-to-follow guide. I do not claim that it will overcome all the problems. No book could. Each one of us is unique, and nowhere is that fact more clearly displayed than in a bundle of CVs where the career patterns of people who have worked in the same trade or profession can be infinitely variable.

Views vary about the layout of a CV, but the method shown in these pages has achieved outstanding results, time and time again.

First, read Part 3 carefully right through. Then, return to this page and start composing the CV. Read a bit and do a bit, then read a bit more and so on, to the end.

I start by showing an unrealistically simple, completed specimen CV. This deliberate over-simplification brings the essential points to the force.

PERSONAL DETAILS

Full Name:	Sarah Jones
Address:	101 Heron Road, Anytown, Midshire, XX1 1YY
Telephone No:	Anytown (01888) 888888
Date of Birth:	9th August (year)
Place of Birth:	Anytown, Midshire
Nationality:	British
Marital Status:	Single – no children
Driving Licence:	Current (clean)

CURRICULUM VITAE

EDUCATION AND QUALIFICATIONS

Sept. (year)	Anytown Comprehensive School,
– July (year)	Anytown, Midshire

June (year) GCSE

Mathematics	(A)
English	(B)
(Oral Communication	2)
Business Studies	(B)
Information Technology	(B)
Geography	(C)
History	(C)

Sept. (year)	Anytown College of Further and Higher
– June (year)	Education, Anytown, Midshire
	– Evening Classes

Royal Society of Arts
June (year) RSA 1 – Word Processing

National Vocational Qualification
June (year)
NVQ Level 3 – Business Administration

TRAINING

Acme Retail Ltd

Oct. (year)	Induction	(1 week)
Nov. (year)	Stock Ordering	(1 day)
Jan. (year)	Office Procedures	(3 days)

EXPERIENCE

Oct. *(year)*
– *to date*

Acme Retail Ltd
66–68 High Street, Anytown, Midshire
– Retailers of Ladies' Fashions

Administration Clerk – daily updating
of sales charts; completing stock
discrepancy forms; balancing tills;
banking; ordering stationery; processing
correspondence.

Apr. *(year)*
– *Oct. (year)*

Porter & Clegg Ltd
Beacon Road, Crossley Industrial
Estate, Anytown, Midshire
– Wholesalers of Paint and Wall
Coverings

Assistant Stock Control Clerk –
checking incoming stock; verifying
invoices; typing customer invoices;
assisting with preparations for audits.

July *(year)*
– *Apr. (year)*

Anytown Estates
90 Leamington Road, Anytown,
Midshire
– Estate Agents and Valuers

Trainee Clerk.

OUTSIDE ACTIVITIES

Hobbies   Walking, aerobics and dancing.

References   Available on request.

15

Personal Details

We will begin by dealing with this section of the CV, not only because it comes first, but also because with all CVs the arrangement of the personal details will be similar. Any differences are confined to the amount of information given.

For instance, where the applicant intends to apply for employment in a particular role, e.g. electrician, the personal details will contain the firm statement that that is what he is, and the fact will then be displayed thus:

Occupation: Electrician – JIB Approved.

The purpose behind this inclusion is to make the reader aware at an early stage that here is a specialist, and not a jack-of-all-trades prepared to try his hand at anything. But beware, because if it is anticipated that a broad range of vacancies might be applied for, the CV may not serve its purpose with the occupation inserted, and the applicant could find himself severely restricted. If this seems likely, no occupation should be included in the personal details.

If the CV is being prepared with a view to applying for a single job vacancy, and is not likely to be used again in the foreseeable future, the applicant's age will appear alongside date of birth. This will reduce the reading time, by eliminating the need for the reader to test his powers of mental arithmetic.

When the CV is likely to be used over a long period, the actual age should not be inserted because the passage of time will eventually create an inaccuracy. Although, if you keep your CV on a word processor/computer you can, of course, update it each time you send it out. However, remember that companies and recruitment agencies frequently hold CVs on file for many months before making a response, so any ages given will go out-of-date.

Although of less importance, the entry giving details about the number and ages of children can also become out-of-date. For this reason, some applicants prefer to give the children's dates of birth only.

Next of kin is a detail which can be needed, particularly if dangerous work or employment overseas is the goal. This is most appropriate in the case of a single or divorced person.

Another sub-heading which might not be used in every instance covers state of health. This applies if physical fitness is likely to be a consideration of more than average importance, e.g. a physical training instructor at a holiday camp, or any post demanding prolonged physical exertion, particularly in climates where extremes of temperature prevail.

Ideally, this aspect of the personal details will be dealt with by declaring the possession of a current medical certificate. People whose leisure pursuits require them to have regular medical checks might also hold a certificate of fitness.

Medical Certificate: Valid to August (year).

Or if no medical certificate is available, the entry will read:

Health: Excellent

(Assuming, of course, that the physical state accords with the entry.)

Showing that the driving licence is clean can say something about a person, and not just that he has had luck on his side. If the job being applied for involves using a company vehicle, a clean licence can be a positive advantage. If the licence is not free from points, the entry will read: Current (full) – assuming that a full licence has been obtained.

If the subject wishes it to be known that he is prepared to relocate, a sub-heading entitled Preferred Location will be included. This might say: Prepared to relocate within the UK. Alternatively, if the applicant wishes to leave open the question of relocation, but desires to enhance his prospects of an interview, he might say: Prepared to work anywhere in the UK, thus leaving himself free to state on some future occasion that he will travel home each weekend. However, it is by no means certain that a prospective employer would accept the latter as an alternative to relocation.

Many people seek work abroad for a variety of reasons. Preferred location might then read: Prepared to work anywhere in the world. Obviously, the question of returning home each weekend would not usually arise in this case. Those who wish to work abroad, but have no previous experience, would do well to remember the reaction of the gentleman who, having returned from a winter in the Falkland Islands, amended his preferred location to read: Prepared to work in any warm country.

Where the applicant does not wish to relocate, under any circumstances, preferring to work within commuting distance, the preferred location sub-heading should not be used.

Sometimes more details are needed. Try to remember the requirements of application forms relating to your own trade, profession or aspirations. For example, in certain foreign parts an applicant may be required to declare his religion. To minimise the risk of a clash of religious beliefs, most seasoned campaigners to foreign parts simply put Christian, and leave it at that.

The national insurance number is always an inclusion

when the CV is being used to apply for work offshore. Again, it is a matter of knowing your own field.

Apart from the items already discussed, the personal details should be presented as in the example below. To some readers, this list may appear to be inordinately large. The reason for its apparent bulk is the need for me to display all the sub-headings which are likely to appear in a CV. It goes almost without saying that few, if any, applicants will require them all. For instance, a person who does not possess a passport is not expected to insert the appropriate sub-heading only to leave a blank space alongside. Neither will he use the passport sub-heading, if he is not likely to be going abroad in his work.

PERSONAL DETAILS

Full Name:	James Smith
Occupation:	Electrician – JIB Approved
Address:	1 The Close, Anytown, Midshire, XX1 1YY
Telephone No:	Anytown (01888) 888888
Date of Birth:	15th February (year). (Age – XX.)
Place of Birth:	Anytown, Midshire
Nationality:	British
Religion:	Christian
Marital Status:	Married with son aged 11 and daughter aged 6.
Next of Kin:	Mrs A Smith (wife) – address as above.
Nat. Ins. No:	ZZ 00 00 00 Z
Driving Licence:	Current (full)
Passport No:	X 88888 Y – expires October (year)
Health:	Excellent
Preferred Location:	Prepared to work anywhere in the world.

16

Education, Qualifications And Training

Like the career details, this section varies from one individual to the next. I have constructed these five examples in such a way as to cover the essentials that all applicants will need.

Education, from the age of eleven onward, should be included. It is common for an applicant to have attended more than one school during these years, therefore we might commence with:

EDUCATION AND QUALIFICATIONS

Sept. (year)	Anytown Comprehensive School
– July (year)	Anytown, Midshire
Sept. (year)	Hightown High School
– July (year)	Hightown, Midshire

Where an applicant has attended more than two schools (I once had a client who had been to nine), it is standard practice to include only the last two.

After showing the school or schools attended, we come to the examination successes and might then proceed as follows:

June (year) GCSE

Mathematics	(C)
English	(C)
(Oral Communication	2)
Home Economics	(C)
Computer Studies	(D)
Physics	(D)
Biology	(E)

Those born before 1972, should give their GCE 'O' Level and/or CSE subjects with grades.

It is generally preferable to present these lists in descending order of grades or pass, although where a particular subject, or subjects, is of greater importance in relation to the kind of work being sought it may be prudent to depart from this practice.

An applicant who has received no further formal training would proceed to the presentation of his career history. However, for the benefit of those who have gone on to further education, we will continue.

Sept. (year)   Anytown College of Further and Higher
– June (year)   Education, Anytown, Midshire
                 – Full-time

(Unlike this course, others might require only part-time attendance, e.g. Day Release, Block Release or Evening Classes – state which.)

> *June (year) BTEC National Diploma*
> *– Hotel, Catering and Institutional Operations*
> (17 Units: 3 Distinctions; 12 Merits; 2 Passes)

> *June (year) BTEC HND*
> *– Hotel, Catering and Institutional Management*
> (18 Units: 10 Merits; 8 Passes)

Where a long list of certificates and diplomas has been obtained, the question sometimes arises: need all of them be listed, or does the final one or possibly the last two outweigh the earlier ones to the point of making them superfluous? This is a question which the applicant will often be able to answer himself. If not, specialist advice should be sought and where doubt still remains, all certificates should be listed. In the case of the HND which we are dealing with here, it is necessary to decide whether it would be worthwhile providing a breakdown of the programme, listing the units passed with the grade of pass obtained in each unit. Whatever the particular field of endeavour may be, this question will always arise with regard to the most advanced qualification gained, because in most cases the recipient of the CV will have little or no knowledge of the course content.

All right, so what do we do? In this instance, I would first find out if the applicant possessed the level of experience to match his HND. If he did, I would prefer to leave things as they stand and use the space saved on the CV to expand on his career history. If he did not possess an adequate range and depth of experience, I would list the units passed, taking them together with the levels and grades of pass straight off the diploma, or its accompanying notification of performance. The need to do this is most common where applicants are of a young age, and have not had the time to develop their careers to any great extent. When facing this dilemma, many applicants place photocopies of their certificates and associated documentation in the envelope with their CV. The resulting bulge of unsolicited material is likely to discourage the recruiter, whose desk may already be piled high with the efforts of others. Far better to have an extra page on the CV, which might at least command respect on account of the time and patience that has obviously been required.

Industrial placements or college placements, whatever their duration, should be treated as a normal job in the career history, with the fact clearly stated in each case, e.g.:

143

June (year) *– Sept.* *(year)*	The George Hotel 125 South Promenade, Anytown, Midshire – Fully licensed residential hotel (45 bedrooms – en suite). Management Trainee on industrial placement. Receptionist – receiving guests; handling telephone enquiries; operating a computerised reservations and accounts system.

If the HND was obtained some years ago, it may not be necessary to include the industrial placements, on account of the experience now gained.

> *Royal Institute of Public Health and*
> *Hygiene*
> *June (year)*
> The Food Hygiene and Handling
> Certificate

Even if this was obtained before the HND, it will come as the last entry in education and qualifications, in order to avoid interrupting the flow of OND and HND information.

Over the years, many applicants will have attended short training courses, run either by the employing company or a specialist training organisation. Where these are at all likely to have a bearing on future employment, they should be included at this point on the CV.

TRANSING

TRAINING

	Global Hotels plc	
June (year)	Organising Functions	(1 week)
Jan. (year)	Interviewing	(3 days)
Feb. (year)	Problem Analysis	(1 week)

It is worth mentioning here, that recruitment agencies tend to rely on key words and phrases when retrieving potential candidates from their databases, e.g. AUTO-CAD, TQM, BS 5750, just-in-time, etc. Sometimes relevant courses (involving these key words) will have been attended, so it is important to include them. Where the involvement has been by way of practical experience, the inclusion will go into the career history section.

This tendency to use key words seems to be most common in the very broad field of engineering, but whatever the occupation, it is a good idea to try and keep pace with the latest techniques and terminology, especially if the CV is going to agencies.

Where an applicant is a member of a professional association, the appropriate entry should be made here, e.g.:

Professional Association
MHCIMA

Where this entry is applicable, it is worth considering whether to include the letters of the professional association alongside your full name in personal details. Although some applicants think it might appear boastful, doing this does convey an instant message to the reader. The same consideration should be given in the case of a degree, e.g. BA (Hons).

This applicant's education, qualifications and training section is now complete, as follows:

EDUCATION AND QUALIFICATIONS

Sept. (year)	Anytown Comprehensive School
– July (year)	Anytown, Midshire
Sept. (year)	Hightown High School
– July (year)	Hightown, Midshire

June (year) GCSE
Mathematics   (C)
English   (C)

(Oral Communication	2)
Home Economics	(C)
Computer Studies	(D)
Physics	(D)
Biology	(E)

Sept. (year) Anytown College of Further and Higher
– June (year) Education, Anytown, Midshire
– Full-time

> *June (year) BTEC National Diploma*
> *– Hotel, Catering and Institutional*
> *Operations*
> (17 Units: 3 Distinctions; 12 Merits;
> 2 Passes)

> *June (year) BTEC HND*
> *– Hotel, Catering and Institutional*
> *Management*
> (18 Units: 10 Merits; 8 Passes)

> *Royal Institute of Public Health and*
> *Hygiene*
> *June (year)*
> The Food Hygiene and Handling
> Certificate

TRAINING

	Global Hotels plc	
June (year)	Organising Functions	(1 week)
Jan. (year)	Interviewing	(3 days)
Feb. (year)	Problem Analysis	(1 week)

Professional Association
MHCIMA

Next comes the less typical case of the applicant whose
further education and training is a mix between civilian

146

and military. Anyone who has served in HM Armed Forces should find this example helpful:

EDUCATION AND QUALIFICATIONS

Sept. (year) *– July (year)*	Anytown School Anytown, Midshire

June (year) CSE

Technical Drawing	(2)
Mathematics	(2)
English	(4)

Sept. (year) *– June (year)*	Anytown College of Technology, Anytown, Midshire – Day Release

City and Guilds of London Institute
– Heavy and Light Vehicle Maintenance
June (year) Part One Certificate
June (year) Part Two Certificate

(Year) – *(year)*	Royal Air Force (Service Qualifications) *(Year)*

Education Test Certificate – Part Two
– English; Geography; History.

TRAINING

(Year)	Instructional Techniques. Forward Reporting. Recruiting. Emergency Services Vehicle Maintenance. Basic Computing.

Setting out the education and qualifications in the way I have shown, i.e. displaying the qualifications immediately below the school, college, university or other establishment at which they were gained, is unfortunately not always practicable. When an applicant has attended numerous colleges and gained separate qualifications at each one, the list becomes so spread out that it has to be handled differently, albeit less satisfactorily:

EDUCATION

Sept. (year) *– July (year)*	Anytown Comprehensive School Anytown, Midshire
Sept. (year) *– June (year)*	Anytown College of Further and Higher Education, Anytown, Midshire – Full-time
Sept. (year) *– June (year)*	Hightown College of Further and Higher Education, Hightown, Midshire – Day Release and Evening Classes
Oct. (year) *– June (year)*	Anytown University Anytown, Midshire – Full-time

QUALIFICATIONS

June (year) GCE 'O' Level

Mathematics	(A)
English Language	(B)
Physics	(B)
History	(B)
Art and Design	(B)
Geography	(C)
French	(D)

June (year) ONC – Electronics
(18 Units: 8 Merits; 5 Passes; 5 Exempt)

June (year) HNC – Electronics
(10 Units: 2 Distinctions; 6 Merits;
2 Passes)

Obviously, the aim here is to economise on space, while still providing the necessary information. However, the question still arises of whether or not to give a course breakdown of the most advanced qualification, in this instance, a degree. In making this decision, you have to bear in mind that the syllabus of one institution may vary from that of another, in the same subject. Unless the recipient of the CV has copies of the different syllabuses readily to hand, confusion could arise. Advice on this should be available to those attending university.

The example shown below assumes that the applicant has graduated from university with a degree in law and is applying for a training contract, prior to attending law school. This applicant provides a year by year breakdown of the degree course.

EDUCATION AND QUALIFICATIONS

Sept. (year) Anytown School
– July (year) Anytown, Midshire

June (year) GCSE
English (A)
(Oral Communication 1)
Mathematics (A)
English Literature (B)
Geography (B)
History (B)
Biology (B)
Chemistry (C)

June (year) GCE 'A' Level
Economics (A)
English (A)
General Studies (B)
Geography (C)

149

Oct. (year) *– June (year)*	University of Anyborough
	June (year) LLB (Hons) – II (ii)

1st Year
English Legal System; Tort; Contract
Law; Criminal Law; Constitutional
Law.

2nd Year
Land Law; Equity and Trusts; Industrial
Law; Administrative Law.

3rd Year
Jurisprudence; Remedies; Family Law;
Civil Liberties.

Sept (year) *– July (year)*	To attend Midshire College of Law. (Legal Practice Course)

Occasionally, the education, qualifications and training might be set out in yet another way, because of the differing make up of the information, e.g.:

EDUCATION

Sept. (year) *– July (year)*	Anytown Comprehensive School Anytown, Midshire

QUALIFICATIONS

Nov. (year)	CITB Advanced Scaffolder's Card – Reg No: XXXXXX
Feb. (year)	NJC/ECI Registered Scaffolder No: XXXXXX
Aug. (year)	Permit User's Certificate No: XXXXXX
June (year)	TJIT Offshore Survival Certificate No: XXXXXX

TRAINING

Cann Scaffolding (Anytown) Ltd

Sept. (year)   Height Awareness (3 days)
Feb. (year)   Health and Safety (1 day)

The reason for the above layout is that there are no purely academic qualifications. This applicant's qualifications are a confirmation of the standards he is able to work to, and of his ability to survive an involuntary dip in the sea.

The preceding five examples of the different ways of approaching the task of setting out the education, qualifications and training section of a CV should provide a suitable structure for the majority of readers.

17

The Career History
Part One

The career history is usually the part of a CV which most
interests the reader. It is also the greatest in its demands of
time, thought and patience on the part of the applicant.

You need to highlight the main duties and responsibilities
of each job, and emphasise any notable achievements.

It is important to stick to the hard facts and to avoid
small-talk, or statements which are merely conversational.
Remember that the CV initially will get no more than a
quick scan, perhaps lasting less than twenty seconds. Upon
the impression given by that first acquaintance with the
recruiter rests the decision as to whether the CV is placed on
the small pile for a longer read later, or simply consigned to
the waste-bin. Elegant flowing prose will impress no-one.
The experienced recruiter will see straight through it and
toss it aside with contempt.

There follow seven career history examples, each one
followed by a question and answer table. Reading all of
the examples should prove helpful to any applicant. It is
important to understand the general style before applying
the principles to your own history.

Do not use the first person (I/we). Thus you greatly
reduce the risk of appearing immodest, and can make a
strong, factual and concise presentation.

A LICENSEE

EXPERIENCE/ACHIEVEMENTS

Feb. (year)
– to date

The Plough Hotel (Anyone's Brewery)
Foxglove Road, Anytown, Midshire
– 28 bedrooms (en suite)
– 2 licensed bars
– A la carte restaurant (80 covers)
– Functions room

Licensed Manager responsible to the
Area Manager for the day-to-day
running of the business, including the
recruitment, training and control of staff
(32); organising weddings, parties,
business conferences and Rotary
functions for up to 120.

ACHIEVEMENT: Through improving
public relations, making staff changes
and applying tighter controls in all areas,
a 15% increase in profitability was
recorded in the first full year. This has
been maintained.

June (year)
– Feb. (year)

The Ship Tavern (Everyone's Brewery)
Beach Road, Anytown, Midshire
– 3 licensed bars
– Dining-room with fast-food and full
meals service (60 covers)

Licensed Manager responsible to the
District Sales Manager for running the
operation, including book-keeping,
control of stock and cash and recruitment
and training of staff (28). Catered for
weddings, funerals, birthday parties and
charity functions for up to 100.

Mar. (year) *– June (year)*	The White Lady Bars and Leisure Complex (Town House Leisure Co Ltd) The Promenade, Anytown, Midshire

Bars Manager responsible for running
this busy, sea-front, multi-bar operation.
Public Bar: Up to 300 customers,
demanding a rapid flow of alcoholic and
soft drinks, as well as bar snacks.
Lounge Bar: Customers comprised a
mixed concentration of locals and
holidaymakers.
Cocktail Bar: Heavy lunch-time and late
evening trade, from professional and
business people.

Responsible for stock control and
acquisition. Thirty-four full and
part-time bar staff and cleaners.

Apr. (year) *– Mar.* *(year)*	The Manor Grill-Room Restaurant Olde Road, Anytown, Midshire – 75 covers – 1 licensed bar

Assistant Manager responsible for
helping the Manager to achieve his
objectives, and deputising in his
absence.
Twenty-two full and part-time staff.

Aug. (year) *– Apr. (year)*	The Dog and Duck Inn (Middle West Brewery), Orchard Lane, Anytown, Midshire – Public House (3 bars)

Bartender – serving beers, shorts and
cocktails to customers from all levels of
society.

155

May (year) *– Aug. (year)*	Unemployed.
Nov. (year) *– May (year)*	The Black Owl (Mountain Brewery) Anytown, Midshire – Fully licensed residential hotel – 55 bedrooms (en suite) Commis Chef – veg, larder and sweet.
Nov. (year) *– Nov. (year)*	The Olde Hall Inn (Free House) Hall Lane, Anytown, Midshire Trainee Cellarman.
July (year) *– Nov. (year)*	Anytown Box Co Ltd Shore Road, Anytown, Midshire Trainee Box Maker.

OUTSIDE ACTIVITIES

Hobbies	Football, squash and reading.
References	Available on request.

Question: *Why does the career history read backwards?*

Answer: Because the present post will be of most interest to the reader, who will want to be able to form an accurate picture of the past ten years.

Question: *In his two most recent jobs, the applicant gives the job title of the person to whom he is responsible. In the other jobs he does not. Why?*

Answer: Because in those two jobs he is the manager of the entire site operation, and the reader will want to know how far up the ladder his line of communication reaches.

        In the other jobs it is obvious that he is either responsible to the manager (as in the positions of assistant manager and bars manager), or someone on the premises at assistant manager or supervisor level (as in the position of bartender). As a commis chef, he will be responsible to someone in the kitchen, probably the head chef or duty chef.

        Whatever your role in your work might be, if you feel that additional emphasis can be given to the weight of responsibility that you carry, by including your immediate superior's job title, then go ahead. But remember, it will use up space and reading time.

Question: *This example covers more than ten years' employment. Why bother to go back so far?*

Answer: To show continuity of employment with no unexplained time gaps. Avoid allowing the reader to draw the conclusion that you might have been in prison or had serious health or mental problems for a time. If a period of unemployment took place a few years ago, show it. This is particularly important where the last ten years are concerned.

Question: *What if the applicant is unable to recall the exact starting and finishing dates of his jobs?*

Answer: Do your best to put it all together, complete with month and year, for the past ten years. Beyond that, most applicants will only be able to recall the exact year, especially where many job changes have occurred.

In some cases, it may not be possible to set down all the jobs and employers in the accepted form. But you can still do a précis, as in the next example. (This question is given further coverage at the start of Chapter 21, Problems, Problems.)

A WORKSHOP MANAGER/ DIESEL ENGINE SPECIALIST

EXPERIENCE

Aug. (year) – to date	Bell & Bamber Transport Ltd Anytown Industrial Estate, Anytown, Midshire – 48 tractor units; 66 trailers

Workshop Manager – running the workshop with seven skilled fitters and two office staff. Responsible for staff recruitment; adherence to strict maintenance schedules; 24-hour breakdown rota; acquisition of spares; checking invoices; ensuring compliance with health and safety regulations. Centrally involved in obtaining BS 5750 accreditation for the company.

Jan. (year) *– Aug. (year)*	Wheelways Marine Ltd 124–130 Dock Road, Anytown, Midshire – Road Haulage, Shipping and Warehousing – 150 articulated and rigid vehicles Fitter – repair and maintenance of diesel engines, transmissions, bodywork and trailers.
Oct. (year) *– Jan. (year)*	Unemployed.
Mar. (year) *– Oct. (year)*	Rance & Leigh Construction (International) Plc, (Engineering and Plant Division), Hounds Road, Anytown, Midshire – Bangassou, Central Africa Workshop Foreman in charge of twenty-eight mechanics, engaged in the repair and maintenance of all heavy and light vehicles on a dam and irrigation project. Ordered all spares; dealt with all workshop documentation.
Sept. (year) *– Mar.* *(year)*	Western Road Services Ltd Town Road, Anytown, Midshire – Road Haulage Contractors (22 rigid vehicles) Foreman Fitter – routine maintenance of commercial vehicles.
Jan. (year) *– Sept.* *(year)*	Smith, Jones & Co Ltd Bridgend Garage, Ford Lane, Anytown, Midshire – Commercial Vehicle Distributors

Fitter – servicing new trucks.

(Year)
– (year)   Hillside Haulage and Repairs Ltd
Down Road, Anytown, Midshire

Diesel Mechanic – all types of
commercial vehicle repairs.

(Year)
– (year)   UK & Foreign Technical Contracts
Employers Ltd, Capetown, South Africa
– South Africa and the Congo Basin

Diesel Mechanic – maintaining heavy
vehicles engaged on dams, bridges, road
works and forest clearance.

(Year)
– (year)   Diesel Mechanic with numerous
companies including:

ABC Haulage Ltd
Rock Street, Anytown, Midshire

Move & Dump Ltd
Ashdown Street, Anytown, Midshire

Joe's Waste Disposal
Smith's Yard, Anytown, Midshire

Fire Engine Breakers and Renovations
Ltd
Anytown, Midshire

West Midshire County Council
(Highways and Technical Services)

(Year)
– (year)   Anytown Construction Services Ltd
(Plant Division), Arkwright Road,
Anytown, Midshire

Apprentice Mechanic (Indentured)
learning all aspects of diesel powered
vehicle and plant repair and
maintenance.

OUTSIDE ACTIVITIES

Hobbies   Cricket and vintage car restoration.

References   Available on request.

Question: *Will it not be damaging to the applicant's
chances to have had so many jobs?*

Answer: To have had few jobs over a long period
of time obviously shows a degree of
stability and reliability, although skilled
tradesmen who have had numerous
employers have usually worked in places
far apart and are accustomed to changes
in working environment. This, coupled
with the broad experience gained, will in
many instances enhance their prospects.

Applicants should seek out jobs which
match their CV.

Question: *Nowhere does this applicant give his
reason for leaving. Why is this?*

Answer: While most job application forms
request the answer to this question, it is
unlikely the truth will always be told,
especially in the case of the applicant
who might have given his employer a
black eye!

It is more effective to leave the reader
with the impression that each job was
superior to the previous one. Unfortunately, this is not always the case.

In the final analysis it is a matter for the individual to decide, but in stating the reason for leaving one job, he could feel obliged to do so for them all.

It is also as well to remember that whatever goes into a CV must be the truth, since it is a criminal offence to obtain employment by deception.

Question: *Why does the career history of this second example come under the heading Experience when in the previous one it came under Experience/Achievements?*

Answer: In the previous example, a particular achievement was singled out for special mention.

Question: *Why is the nature of the employer's business not fully stated every time?*

Answer: Where the nature of a company's business activities is adequately conveyed in the company name, to elaborate further would be a waste of space and reading time.

AN ELECTRICIAN – SEEKING WORK OFFSHORE

EXPERIENCE

June (year) *– to date*	Anytown Management Services Ltd – Contracting to Cann Oil
	Approved Electrician on Cann 'B' Platform – installation of electrical fire and gas systems.

May (year) *– June (year)*	Broadvale Engineering, Anytown Approved Electrician on Morecambe Bay hook-up – installation and commissioning of fire and gas instrumentation; running and terminating cables; wiring PA systems; ladder racking and tray work.
Feb. (year) *– May (year)*	RCN Electrical Contractors (Anytown) Ltd – Midchester Leisure Centre Approved Electrician – installation of heavy gauge cable trunking.
Nov. (year) *– Feb. (year)*	AMA Nuclear Systems Plc – Norsham Power Station Approved Electrician – installation and testing of thermo-couples, strain gauges and microphones.
Mar. (year) *– Nov. (year)*	Hall & Rowe Ltd, Anytown – New hypermarket for C&J Approved Electrician – installation of EPOS computer systems, emergency lighting, via contractor controls; automatic doors; zone fire alarm systems; steel wire armoured cable.
Sept. (year) *– Mar. (year)*	BDR Construction (UK) Ltd – Saudi Arabian Hospital Building Contract Approved Electrician – installation of floor trunking and sockets; all theatre electrification; fire alarms; smoke and gas detection equipment.

June (year)	T & G Electrics (Anytown) Ltd
– Sept. (year)	

June (year) – September (year)
Electrician/Approved Electrician.

June (year) – June (year)
Apprentice Electrician (Indentured).

OUTSIDE ACTIVITIES

Hobbies   Keep Fit, Home Computing and DIY.

References   Available on request.

Question: *Why does this applicant not give the full
addresses of his employers? Sometimes, he
only gives the company's name.*

Answer: He is applying for work in the offshore oil
and gas industry where recruitment staff
will know most, if not all, of the
companies shown in the CV.
Furthermore, this industry is one of the
most demanding in its need for a brief, but
informative document.

Some of my clients even prefer not to
use valuable space on items such as
outside activities, or the mention of
references. But that is their decision.

Where the applicant has limited
offshore experience or none at all, he
should give the addresses and main
business activities of his employers in the
usual way. His outside activities and his
ability to provide references should also
be shown briefly, as in the above example.
The length of a CV is given further
coverage on page 242 in Chapter 21,
Problems, Problems.

Question: *Why bother to say that the apprenticeship was indentured?*

Answer: The quality of training given to apprentices varies and the possession of indentures (increasingly rare) will give a prospective employer more confidence, especially so in the case of a young applicant.

A MOTOR MECHANIC

– newly discharged from HM Armed forces and seeking work in civilian life.

EXPERIENCE

Oct. (year)
– May (year)

Army – Royal Electrical and Mechanical Engineers.

July (year) – May (year)
Section Commander (UK) responsible for acquisition, control and inspection of all high and low cost items used in the repair and maintenance of tracked military vehicles.
Twenty subordinate fitters and technicians.

April (year) – July (year)
Section Commander (Germany) – inspection and testing of wheeled military vehicles and the control and inspection of workshop equipment.

June (year) – April (year)
Corporal Mechanic (UN Forces – Cyprus) – control and acquisition of vehicle and equipment spare parts. Up to five subordinates.

October (year) – June (year)
Mechanic working in UK and Germany, carrying out major repairs to heavy plant. Much of this work was done in field conditions, where inaccessibility demanded frequent improvisation.

October (year) – October (year)
REME School – as above. [This will have been included in Education, Qualifications and Training.]

Certificate of Service reads: Conduct Exemplary
Rank on Discharge: Corporal.

Sept. (year) – Oct. (year)	Bardale Auto Services Ltd 19–21 Avon Road, Anytown, Midshire Apprentice Motor Mechanic – full-time in the workshop while awaiting REME service.
Summary	Extensive experience gained on a wide range of light and heavy vehicles: petrol, diesel, tracked and 4 × 4. Arc, MIG and oxyacetylene welding. Fitting and turning. Refrigeration. Air conditioning. DC generators.

Objective	To become a Commercial Vehicle Workshop Manger.

OUTSIDE ACTIVITIES

Hobbies	Snooker and fell walking.
References	Available on request.

Question: *This example shows that the applicant's most recent job has terminated, therefore he must be unemployed. Is that not going to jeopardise his chances?*

Answer: Unfortunately yes, and the longer he remains unemployed the worse his plight will become. He must proceed immediately to go flat out to find a job. Even if the new job does not ideally match what he is looking for, it will get him back on the ladder and provide a firmer platform from which to apply for something more suitable.

Question: *Is it always a good idea to provide a summary of experience in this way?*

Answer: Only if you feel that the descriptions of your jobs cannot be made to convey enough of this kind of information without becoming too bulky. This question occurs most often with ex-Armed Forces and Merchant Navy personnel.

Question: *The Objective has not been included in previous examples. Why not?*

Answer: Because, as with Occupation in the personal details, a declared Objective could be binding if the applicant is likely to apply for a wide range of jobs.

Service in the Armed Forces will sometimes have been so involved that attempting to break it down into a conventional presentation would be impracticable. In such cases, a short narrative can be the best approach. E.g:

EXPERIENCE

Oct. (year) *– May (year)*	Army – Royal Electrical and Mechanical Engineers.

After twelve months at the REME School of Mechanical Engineering, a variety of postings in the UK and Germany involved the servicing and repair of heavy plant. Then followed a three year period as a Corporal Mechanic, serving with the UN Forces in Cyprus, in control of vehicle and parts acquisition.

Became a Section Commander in (year), with responsibility for the inspection and testing of wheeled military vehicles, and for the control and inspection of work-shop equipment.

On returning to the UK in (year), the number of subordinate personnel increased from five to twenty. Additional responsibilities included the control and inspection of a wide variety of high and low cost items, as well as the repair, maintenance and testing of wheeled and tracked vehicles.

Certificate of Service reads: Conduct
Exemplary.
Rank on Discharge: Corporal.

Question: *Should a summary be attached where this
approach is made?*

Answer: Yes, when the applicant is still engaged
in the same type of work.

Question: *Might it not be a good idea to present an
Armed Forces career in this way, even if it
is not long and complicated?*

Answer: Yes, but only if it took place some years
previously, and is no longer the main
topic.

A STUDENT

Part-time Work Experience

(Year)   Smith's Newsagents
– (year)   22 Manor Road, Anytown, Midshire

     Morning newspaper round.

(Year)   (Summer holidays)
     Anytown Leisure Ltd
     The Promenade, Anytown, Midshire

     Cashier – handing out change to
customers.

(Year)   (Weekends)
– (year)   Dot's Cake Shop
     14 Belgrave Road, Anytown, Midshire

Sales Assistant – selling bread and cakes, as well as helping in the bakery.

(Year)	(Weekends and Summer holidays)
– (year)	Anytown Stables
	Church Road, Anytown, Midshire

Stable Yard Assistant – grooming, cleaning out and exercising horses.

Additional Information

School:
Prefect.
Captain of Netball Team and member of Hockey Team.
Duke of Edinburgh Award Scheme – Silver Award.

University:
Treasurer of the Anytown University Fund for Distressed Former Students.

OUTSIDE ACTIVITIES

Hobbies All animals – particularly horses. Comic Opera.

References Available on request.

Question: *Is it not a good idea to enclose copies of testimonials or names of referees with each application?*

Answer: These are not generally enclosed with the CV, but there are exceptions.
  Students and graduates invariably include the name of referees, whether requested to do so or not. Professional people with an established career often

170

do the same, and I am not opposed to this, but remember that the final entry on the CV will then read:

References – Enclosed.

Typing the names and addresses of referees (usually two, sometimes three), onto a separate sheet for photocopying, is preferable to including them on the last page of the CV, because changing or adding one at a later date will not then interfere with the CV itself.

A minority of people possess written testimonials from previous employers. Where these are outstanding in their praise of an individual's integrity and competence, I usually recommend enclosing the best two, whatever the person's trade or profession might be.

Question: *Unlike earlier examples, the career history does not run in reverse, and the exact starting and finishing dates are not shown. Why?*

Answer: It can be a good idea for a young person to show clearly that he started work as soon as he was old enough, rather than having waited until he had no choice in the matter.

As for starting and finishing dates, obviously the whole working period would be constantly interrupted by academic pursuits.

Question: *Is it wise for someone who might be in the final year of a degree course to admit to having done such jobs?*

Answer: Yes. It is important to display a positive willingness to tackle almost anything.

Question: *Why tell people that you were a school prefect or a games captain?*

Answer: Positions held at school can sometimes influence the reader's attitude, especially where the applicant sees himself as a suitable candidate for a position requiring self-motivation and the ability to shoulder heavy responsibility.

To have been a school prefect is an indicator pointing in the right direction. A house captain or captain of a school team, e.g. football, cricket, athletics, netball, etc., indicates a degree of leadership quality. To have been a member of a school team or teams suggests an ability to function in harmony with others.

Positions held at university are worthwhile inclusions, provided they do not appear so time consuming that the reader might gain the impression that the applicant has his priorities in the wrong order.

Question: *Why is part-time work not shown in all CVs?*

Answer: When a full-time career has been established, it is likely to overshadow anything that has gone before, although some part-time work may still be worth including, e.g. Territorial Army weekend service. This would come under Outside Activities, as would voluntary work in aid of charity, or perhaps the St John Ambulance Brigade.

Further coverage concerning part-time work will be found on page 236 in Chapter 21, Problems, Problems.

AN ESTATE AGENT

EXPERIENCE/ACHIEVEMENTS

Feb. (year)
– to date

Anytown Estates Ltd
105-107 High Street, Anytown, Midshire
– Estate Agents and Valuers
(5 branches)

September (year) – to date
Branch Manager (Hightown Branch) responsible to the Financial Director for the day-to-day running of the branch, with its high volume Midchester Building Society agency.

Duties include valuing domestic properties and securing new business; formulating press advertisements and property sales hand-outs; negotiating sales; liaising with solicitors; attending weekly management meetings; on the-job staff training; interviewing and appointing branch staff (3).

ACHIEVEMENT: Exceeded (year) business target by 9.3%, while fees remained at 2% (firm).

February (year) – September (year)
Valuer/Negotiator (Anytown Branch) –
valuing properties; formulating
hand-outs; negotiating sales; liaising
with solicitors; resolving problems.
Assisted with staff recruitment and
deputised in the Manager's absence.

ACHIEVEMENT: Won a weekend for
two in Paris in (year), for the most
improved performance at any of the five
branches.

Apr. (year)   Clock Publishing Ltd
– Feb. (year)   41 Cheapside, Anytown, Midshire
               – Media Publishers

Sales Agent – selling advertising space
on estate agents' folders to tradesmen
and retailers.

July (year)   H & L Music
– Apr. (year) 169 Church Street, Anytown, Midshire
              – Retailers of Records, Cassettes and
              Compact Discs

Sales Assistant – selling; display; stock
control.

OUTSIDE ACTIVITIES

Hobbies   Ornithology.
              Water skiing and rock climbing.

Foreign   French – passable.
Languages

References   Available on request.

174

Question: *This is the first example in which the applicant claims to be able to speak a foreign language, but why say 'passable'?*

Answer: If the applicant is fluent, it should say so on the CV. If the applicant can just get by, it will say 'passable'.

Unless the language in question is spoken reasonably well, it must not be included.

Question: *Why is the employer's post code never shown?*

Answer: Few applicants are able to remember the post codes of past employers.

Question: *What address can I put down if one of my past employers has gone out of business and is no longer there?*

Answer: You are writing a concise account of your career history as it has taken place. The fact that one of your former employers is no longer around is not relevant. The address from which they conducted their business when you worked for them is the address you should use. Alternatively, if they are still in business but have moved to new premises, you could give their current address. This is particularly worthwhile, in the case of a former employer who is likely to give you a favourable recommendation, if approached by a prospective employer.

A REGIONAL SALES MANAGER

EXPERIENCE/ACHIEVEMENTS

Apr. (year)
– to date

Flakey Friend Ltd
126–132 Elephants Walk, Anytown,
Midshire
– Manufacturers and Distributors of
Breakfast Cereals

August (year) – to date
Midland Counties Regional Sales
Manager responsible to the National
Sales Manager, Mr J Jones, for the
profitable growth of business
throughout the region. Responsibilities
cover promotions, distribution and the
effective display of products;
recruitment and development of sales
representatives (8).

ACHIEVEMENT: During this time, a
27% increase in sales (volume) has taken
place and sales targets are consistently
being exceeded by 3%–5%.

March (year) – August (year)
Area Sales Manager responsible to the
Regional Sales Manager for effective
space allocation and promotion of the
company's products.
Six subordinate sales representatives.

ACHIEVEMENT: Consistently
exceeded sales targets, by up to 6%.

April (year) – March (year)
Sales Representative – developing new business throughout the area, and promoting a new product.

ACHIEVEMENT: Awarded an engraved gold watch, presented by the Managing Director in person, in recognition of the success with which the new product had been launched in the area.

June (year)
– Apr. (year)
Wispy Hair Products Ltd
New Road, Anytown, Midshire

Sales Representative – developing the company's business through high street outlets and supermarket chains.

Feb. (year)
– June (year)
The Southern Gas Co
Leigh Road, Anytown, Midshire

Showroom Sales Assistant – selling domestic gas appliances.

July (year)
– Feb. (year)
Anytown Colourings Ltd
Lowe Road, Anytown, Midshire
– Suppliers of Paint and Wallcoverings to the Decorating Trade

Warehouse Assistant – unloading and stacking incoming stock.

OUTSIDE ACTIVITIES

Hobbies   Squash, tennis and making home videos.

References   Available on request.

Question: *Why, on one occasion, does the applicant give the name of the person to whom he is reporting, as well as his job title?*

Answer: Sometimes, a senior company official will be so well respected within the industry that the mere mention of his name could command attention.

Question: *Why do none of the examples disclose the wage or salary?*

Answer: To state the wage or salary being paid in one's present job can be harmful, if it is too far out of line with that of the post being applied for. The danger with stating the earnings level of previous jobs is that the figures would be historic, and the applicant's fortunes would probably depend on the reader's ability to allow for inflation, during the intervening years.

If the job advertisement requests the detail of your current rate of pay, include this in the introductory letter (see page 245).

Question: *Should I ask a third party to pass an opinion on my CV (and letters) before they are sent out?*

Answer: It is a good idea to let someone have a look even if only to check for spelling mistakes. But danger lurks. The urge to criticise is just one facet of human nature, and the chosen party may not feel happy in returning the documents with little, or no comment. The possible consequences are obvious and potentially destabilising. Try to choose someone whose opinions are worth having, but who is not a close acquaintance. This will minimise the risk of intrusion by the individual's emotions, and make an objective appraisal more likely.

18

The Career History
Part Two

A collection of career histories from which outside activities and references available have been omitted, in order to avoid tedious repetition. These should, of course, be included when preparing your own CV.

A PLUMBING AND HEATING ENGINEER

EXPERIENCE

Jan. (year) *– to date*	Bates, Barlow (Construction) Ltd Park House, Eagle Industrial Estate Anytown, Midshire – New 1500 bed teaching hospital in Riyadh, Saudi Arabia
	Foreman Plumber in charge of twenty expatriate tradesmen and up to forty Filipino labourers. Responsible for all pipework including medical gas, water, sprinkler and irrigation systems; completion of weekly time and bonus sheets.

Feb. (year) *– Jan. (year)*	Rance Leigh Construction (International) Plc, Hounds Road, Anytown, Midshire – New 300 bedroomed hotel at Dubai, UAE Foreman Plumber in charge of eight expatriate tradesmen and ten Filipino labourers. Responsible for the installation of kitchen equipment, en suite bathrooms, garden irrigation and sprinkler systems and all related pipework.
Sept. (year) *– Feb. (year)*	Harris Mechanical Services Ltd Abbey Road, Anytown, Midshire – Sports Centre and Shopping Precinct in Muscat, Oman Foreman Plumber in charge of up to fifty expatriate plumbers. Responsible for the installation of galvanised and copper pipework; PVC underground services; sheet-metal ducting; toilets and showers; irrigation pipework.
Mar. (year) *– Sept.* *(year)*	Hull & Blackwell Ltd Tower House, Humber Road, Anytown, Midshire – Industrial Plumbing Contractors – Cann Chemical Factory in Akassa, Nigeria Plumber installing pneumatic and stainless-steel instrument pipework; steam pipework; chemical storage tanks.

June (year) *– Mar.* *(year)*	Anytown Plumbing and Heating Ltd Sidings Road, Anytown, Midshire

Plumber fitting bathrooms and installing pipework on a hotel refurbishment contract. Installing new gas central heating systems and appliances, on conversions of large houses to homes for the elderly.

June (year) *– June (year)*	The Park Plumbing and Heating Co Ltd 61–63 Park Road, Anytown, Midshire

Apprentice Plumber (Indentured).

A HAIRDRESSER

EXPERIENCE/ACHIEVEMENT

Oct. (year) *– to date*	The Boulevard Hair Studio 2 The Boulevard, Anytown, Midshire

Senior Stylist supervising four hairdressers, providing a service to clients of all ages. Working eight to ten hours a day, duties include on-the-job staff training; balancing daily takings; banking; security of premises (key holder).

ACHIEVEMENT: During this two year period, the volume of business has increased by 18%, despite strong competition in the locality.

June (year) *– Oct. (year)*	The Salon in the Sun 24 Church Road, Anytown, Midshire

Senior Stylist supervising one hairdresser and two juniors, providing either a traditional or contemporary service. Duties included selling hair products; designing interior and window displays; stock control; security and banking of takings.

Nov. (year) *– June (year)*	Victor's Hair Studio 47 Hillside, Anytown, Midshire – Ladies' and Men's Hairdressing Salon

Stylist in a team of seven, providing a high standard of service to tourists and local business people.

July (year) *– Nov. (year)*	Mobile Hair Stylist visiting clients at home. Built up an established client list of one hundred and twenty, and gained extensive experience in the products of all major manufacturers.

July (year) *– July (year)*	Anytown Hair Studio 15 Village Walk, Anytown, Midshire

Apprentice Hairdresser.

A BUTCHER

EXPERIENCE

July (year) *– to date*	M H Johnson & Sons (Butchers) Ltd 28 Abbey Road, Anytown, Midshire – Retail Butchers (18 branches)

Shop Manager (Midchester Branch) responsible to the Area Manager for the day-to-day running of the operation and the profitable growth of business, from sales of fresh carcase meat and cooked meats. Duties include the supervision of a butcher and two sales assistants; on-the-job staff training; completing staff time-sheets; the preparation and presentation of carcase meat; purchasing stock; pricing to achieve set margins; daily cash reconciliation; weekly stock-taking and the preparation of weekly trading reports.

Sept. (year)
– July (year)

Bennett's
178 High Street, Anytown, Midshire – Wholesale and Retail Butchers, Sausage and Pie Makers

Butcher/Cutter working in a team of five. Duties included cutting meat for display; arranging window and counter displays; preparing cooked meats, i.e. ham, beef, pork, black puddings and barbecued chickens.

July (year)
– Sept.
(year)

R & H Leigh
64 Shaw Road, Anytown, Midshire – Family Butchers

Butcher – cutting up cows, sheep and pigs; boning and rolling meats; ordering carcases, hams, bacon and fowl; arranging displays; serving customers.

July (year)
– July (year)

F Southworth
95 North Road, Anytown, Midshire – Retail Butchers, Sausage and Pie Makers

Apprentice Butcher learning all aspects of the trade, e.g. cutting, boning and rolling; making sausages, pies, black puddings and potted meat; quality control; costing and pricing; display.

A CAR SALESMAN

EXPERIENCE/ACHIEVEMENTS

Aug. (year)
– to date

Anytown Automotive Ltd
23–27 St Patrick's Road, Anytown, Midshire
– Rover Main Dealers

November (year) – to date
Sales Manager responsible to the Dealer Principal for achieving agreed minimum new vehicle sales figures, and complying with used vehicle sales budgets.
Duties include ordering and control of new vehicle stocks; meeting customer finance targets; control and motivation of five sales staff, four valeters and three office personnel.

ACHIEVEMENTS: 17% increase in unit sales of new vehicles in first year; used vehicle sales consistently ahead of budgets.

August (year) – November (year)
Senior Sales Executive selling new Rover cars and selected used cars.
Duties included developing the business user market; used car appraisals; promoting private and business user funding facilities; compiling sales staff rotas.

ACHIEVEMENT: 67% unit sales increase to business users in the first year.

Apr. (year)
– Aug. (year)

Emerson's (Anytown) Ltd
19–23 High Street, Anytown, Midshire
– Mazda Main Dealers

New and Used Car Salesman/Administrator.
Duties – new and used car sales; used car evaluation; completing finance; insurance and registration documentation; liaison with customer and workshop.

July (year)
– Apr. (year)

J L Jupp (Motors) Ltd
Suffolk Road, Anytown, Midshire
– Lada Main Dealers

Junior Car Salesman learning show-room and office techniques and procedures.

A HEAVY PLANT/CRANE OPERATOR

EXPERIENCE

Oct. (year)
– to date

ABC Plant Hire Ltd
Bridge Street, Anytown, Midshire

Heavy Plant Operator – driving 'dozers, motorscrapers, wheeled shovels and dump trucks in bulk earthwork contracts.
Much site reinstatement work.

Sept. (year) *– Oct. (year)*	Ram International plc Willow Road, Anytown, Midshire – Civil Engineering Contractors Motorway Construction Contract Plant Foreman – liaising with Works Manager; allocation of work to forty drivers operating 'dozers, excavators, loading shovels and dump trucks.
Feb. (year) *– Sept. (year)*	Heave-Ho Ltd Moor Road, Anytown, Midshire – Civil Engineering Contractors Saudi Arabian Airport Contract Heavy Plant Operator – 'dozing and stockpiling demolition rubble; levelling rock; stripping concealed rock for quarries; levelling fill for runway, apron and roads to finished levels; all reinstatement work.
Nov. (year) *– Feb. (year)*	J J Jones Ltd New Street, Anytown, Midshire – Civil Engineering and Building Contractors Contracted to Libyan Government – constructing a new roadway Heavy Plant Operator – driving 'dozers and motorscrapers.
Jan. (year) *– Nov. (year)*	UK & Foreign Technical Services Employers Ltd, 122–128 The Square, Anytown, Midshire Prison Contract for the Nigerian Government Crane/Plant Operator driving mobile and rough terrain cranes on the construction

of steel framed two storey buildings,
with concrete panel cladding.
Driving 'dozers, face shovels and
motorscrapers.

Sept. (year)
– Jan. (year)

ABS Plant Hire Ltd
Turnbull Road, Garth Industrial Estate,
Anytown, Midshire
Cann Oil Refinery Contract

Crane Operator – installation of heavy
machinery; movement and location of
large capacity vessels; lifting steelwork.

Sept. (year)
– Sept.
(year)

Maxisenta (Marine) Ltd
28–34 Dunne Road, Anytown, Midshire
Deep-sea Salvage; Offshore Oil and Gas
Exploration.

Crane Operator (Offshore – North Sea)
on the 'Maxi Driller'.
Duties – loading and unloading supply
vessels; stacking containers; lifting drill
floor equipment. Supervised a six man
deck crew and all loading and unloading
of bulk supplies.

July (year)
– Sept.
(year)

Wolfe Bros (Anytown) Ltd
Hyde Road, Anytown, Midshire
– Steel Stockholders

Crane Operator on mobile and overhead
cranes.

July (year)
– July (year)

J A Smith (Farms) Ltd
Back Lane, Anytown, Midshire

General Farm Worker/Tractor Driver.

A BANK CLERK

EXPERIENCE

Sept. (year) The Moorland Bank Plc
– to date St Bartholomew's Road, Hightown,
Midshire

April (year) – to date
– Anytown Branch

Administration Clerk (Grade 3)
responsible for the effective supervision
of seven correspondence clerks. Duties
include the control of bid deposits; close
checking of suspense account
statements; control of foreign
transactions; balancing of travellers'
cheques; opening and distributing
incoming post; assisting with security
checks and tests, re: premises and
strongroom.

May (year) – April (year)
– Sometown Branch

Administration Clerk (Grade 3) in a
team of three, responsible for securities,
i.e. the charging of mortgages, life
policies, stocks and shares.

June (year) – May (year)
– Moortown Branch

Administration Clerk (Grade 3) – duties similar to Sometown (above), but with frequent relief work. Customers included immigrants with language difficulties, and many business people conducting overseas transactions. Authorised to sanction loan applications up to £1500.

February (year) – June (year)
– Anytown Branch

Administration Clerk (Grade 2) – updating and balancing the general ledger accounts; foreign currency exchange; international payment transfers; counter service.

September (year) – February (year)
– Hightown Branch

Administration Clerk (Grade 1) – computer terminal input of day's transactions; updating savings accounts' pass-books; encoding incoming cheques; dealing with customer enquiries by telephone and in person.

A DANCER

EXPERIENCE

July (year) – Sept. (year)

Summer Extravaganza
The Hippodrome, Anytown, Midshire
– Musical Comedy Show

Dancing in a duo performing three, five-minute, routines.

Dec. (year)	(Christmas Season – six weeks)
– Jan. (year)	The Central Pier Pavilion
	Anytown, Midshire
	– Mother Goose

Dancing five routines twice daily, in a troupe of four. Designed costumes; trained stand-ins; assisted with lighting.

Jan. (year)	Curtain Call Theatrical Agency
– May (year)	Bourne Road, Anytown, Midshire
	– Night Club Contract in Athens

Dancing four, three-minute, solo routines, five nights a week.

July (year)	The Harry and Barry Summer Show
– Sept.	Theatre Royal, Anytown, Midshire
(year)	

Dancing four, five-minute routines, in a troupe of eight, six nights a week. Personally choreographed the routines.

June (year)	The Hotel Sahara Cabaret Bar
– Sept.	East Beach, Anytown, Midshire
(year)	

Solo Dancer performing four, five-minute, routines, five nights a week.

(Year)	The Palace Theatre
– (year)	Anytown, Midshire

Dancer in five Christmas pantomimes (each running for six weeks), i.e. Dick Whittington; Cinderella; Snow White and the Seven Dwarfs; Aladdin; Babes in the Wood.

Promotional work

(Year)	The J A Smith Model Agency
– (year)	9 West Drive, Anytown, Midshire

Promotional assignments for swimwear and soft drinks, Milesmaker F701 Sports Car Launch – photographed with the car, and appeared nationally in four motoring magazines.

A POLICEMAN

– seeking work, following retirement from the Police Service.

EXPERIENCE

Aug. (year)	Midshire Constabulary
– June (year)	

November (year) – June (year)
– Stationed at Anytown South

Collator (Intelligence Officer) responsible for correlating information; organising conferences; liaising with security personnel from local stores and factories; instructing new recruits in intelligence work.

April (year) – November (year)
– Anytown North

Coroner's Office responsible to the Chief Superintendent and the Coroner for all administrative procedures, in relation to deaths referred to the Coroner. Duties included visiting scenes of reported deaths; taking witness statements; deciding on further police action; liaising with pathologists and solicitors; conducting mortuary identifications; liaising with appropriate police departments and government agencies; collating inquest data; completing sudden death forms.

January (year) – April (year)
– Hightown Central

Duty Officer – handling enquiries and complaints in the public office; writing reports; maintaining records; issuing lost property receipts; directing car and foot patrols by radio.

October (year) – January (year)
– Midchester Central

Uniformed Constable running the Traffic Wardens' Ticket Office, i.e. issuing notices to recover payment of overdue fines; maintaining records.

February (year) – October (year)
– Midchester South

Uniformed Constable – responding to 999 calls; attending road traffic accidents; dealing with sudden death situations.

August (year) – February (year)
– Hightown South

Uniformed Constable on foot patrol, following completion of ten week course at Home Office training centre.

A FINANCIAL CONSULTANT

EXPERIENCE/ACHIEVEMENTS

Nov. (year)
– to date

Anytown Financial Services Ltd
London Street, Anytown, Midshire

Financial Consultant visiting potential
clients, identifying client needs and
advising on life assurance, pensions and
investments.

ACHIEVEMENT: Expanded the client
base by 57% in the first year.

Feb. (year)
– Nov. (year)

Eternal Life Assurance Ltd
78–82 High Street, Anytown, Midshire

Area Representative (Hightown)
responsible for selling life assurance,
personal pensions, company pension
plans, investment packages and
endowment mortgages.

ACHIEVEMENT: Never lower than
third in the monthly sales table of
thirty-six area representatives.

Aug. (year)
– Feb. (year)

K E Tagg Associates
21 Leicester Road, Anytown, Midshire
– Insurance Brokers

Client Adviser – dealing with all aspects
of property and motor insurance, i.e.
supplying quotations; amending
policies; processing claims; updating
files; preparing accounts.

Apr. (year) *– Aug. (year)*	Highgate Developments (Anytown) Ltd Greenacres Road, Anytown, Midshire – House Builders

Sales Negotiator – conducting show house viewings; advising on fixtures and fittings; selling sites; liaising with site agent, company's solicitor and vendor's solicitor.

July (year) *– Apr. (year)*	Anytown Estates 105–107 High Street, Anytown, Midshire

Clerk/Receptionist.

A SCAFFOLDER

EXPERIENCE

Jan. (year) *– to date*	MASS Offshore Ltd Steele Road, Anytown, Midshire

Foreman Scaffolder (Offshore – North Sea) on Cann Oil Platform.
Duties – supervising up to thirty scaffolders; assessing jobs and ordering materials; liaising with electricians, riggers and painters; quality control; working to drawings and stress limits; ensuring compliance with health and safety at work regulations; acquiring work permits; completing staff time-sheets and keeping the safety standards book.

Mar. (year) *– Dec. (year)*	Rance Leigh Construction (International) Plc, Hounds Road, Anytown, Midshire – Norsham Nuclear Power Station (Stage II)

Advanced Scaffolder erecting all types of scaffolding, up to 180 ft high.

Aug. (year)
– Mar.
(year)

Standfast Scaffolding Ltd
19 Halls Lane, Anytown, Midshire

December (year) – March (year)
– Cann Chemical Plant Maintenance
Contract

Advanced Scaffolder working in a team
of four, erecting tower and independent
scaffolding.

August (year) – December (year)
– Fox 'C' Nuclear Power Station
Contract

Advanced Scaffolder erecting suspended
scaffolding inside boilers.

May (year)
– Aug. (year)

RLS (Anytown) Ltd
181 London Road, Anytown, Midshire
– Scaffolding Contractors
– Oil Rig Rebuilding Contract – UK and
Holland

Scaffolder working in dry dock, erecting
dropping scaffolds and specially
designed double fitting hangers.

Mar. (year)
– May (year)

A & J Scaffolding Ltd
34 Gorse Road, Anytown, Midshire

Scaffolder on major civil engineering
and building works for retail store
groups, aircraft manufacturers, banks
and churches.

Oct. (year) *– Mar.* *(year)*	Anytown Scaffolding Ltd Bank Commercial Street, Anytown, Midshire

Scaffolder on theatre and factory maintenance contracts, including a fire damaged 150 bedroomed hotel – erected wall scaffold to cantilevers.

July (year) *– Oct. (year)*	Maxisenta Support Services Ltd 36 Dunne Road, Anytown, Midshire – Scaffolding Contractors

July (year) – October (year)
Scaffolder.

July (year) – July (year)
Trainee Scaffolder.

A TEACHER

EXPERIENCE

Sept. (year) *– to date*	St Augustine's High School Anytown, Midshire

English Teacher responsible for taking GCSE and 'A' Level classes.
'A' Level pass rates have exceeded 75%.
Deputised for the Head of Department, for one term, during his absence.
Appointed Housemistress in September (year), in charge of 150 children.

Sept. (year) *– July (year)*	Anytown School Anytown, Midshire – Independent Co-Educational School (Entrance by examination)

English Teacher responsible for teaching fourth and fifth year classes.
Placed in charge of school debating society (three to four topical debates each term, frequently involving other schools).
Drama – supervised two major productions each year.
Arranged and accompanied educational trips to Holland and Germany.

Sept. (year)
– July (year)

Anyborough Comprehensive School
Anyborough, Midshire

English Teacher taking classes to 'O' Level standard.
Extra curricular duties included adapting and directing productions for the school dramatic society.

Sept. (year)
– July (year)

Anytown High School
Anytown, Midshire
– (Now closed and formerly Anytown Grammar School)

English Teacher taking English classes up to 'O' Level standard.
Actively involved in the introduction of Integrated Humanities.

A MARINE ENGINEER

– seeking work on or offshore.

EXPERIENCE

Sept. (year)
– to date

MPD Ships Ltd
93–99 Wharfe Street, Anytown,
Midshire
– General Cargo Ships

October (year) – to date
Second Engineer Officer responsible for
the implementation of a planned
maintenance programme, for the main
propulsion engines and auxiliary power
sources.
Responsibilities include being in charge
of the watch (8 hours), and supervising
the repair and routine maintenance of
refrigeration, air conditioning, water
desalination and oil purification systems.

September (year) – October (year)
Third Engineer Officer responsible for
carrying out weekly tests of Unmanned
Machinery Space alarm systems; repair
and routine maintenance of the electric
steering motors and the diesel powered
electricity generators.

Aug. (year)
– Sept.
(year)

Tank and Container Marine Freighters
Ltd
41–43 Dock Road, Anytown, Midshire
– Crude Oil Tankers and Container
Ships

June (year) – September (year)
Fourth Engineer Officer in charge of the watch.
Responsible for the repair and routine maintenance of compressors, oil purification centrifuges, pumps and related systems.

August (year) – June (year)
Junior Engineer in charge of the auxiliary systems watch.

Aug. (year) – Aug. (year)
Global Tankers Ltd
231–233 Flag Road, Anytown, Midshire – Crude Oil Tankers

Indentured Apprentice Marine Engineer (Cadet).

Summary
Extensive experience gained with:

Low and medium speed, 2 and 4 stroke diesel engines up to 30,000 bhp.
Diesel powered generators up to 1,500 kW.
Low-pressure water tube boilers and related water treatment processes.
Water desalination.
Oil purification.
Refrigeration and air conditioning.
Hydraulic systems up to 2,000 PSI working pressure.
Air compressors.
Centrifugal and screw pumps.
Milling and turning.
Gas and arc welding.

A MANAGING DIRECTOR

EXPERIENCE/ACHIEVEMENTS

Mar. (year)   Baldwin, Barker & Co (Anytown) Ltd
– to date   86 Tower Gate, Anytown, Midshire
               – Property Investment and Development

July (year) – to date
Managing Director responsible to the
Chairman for instant decision making
and the day-to-day running of the
company; liaising with company
architects, solicitors, accountants and
bankers, in the planning and execution of
developments, up to £3.5 million.
Responsibilities include scrutinising main
contractors' returned tender documents
and presiding at high-level meetings.
Regular liaison with co-directors covering
sales, purchases and leases.

ACHIEVEMENT: Through encouraging
an improved performance from existing
staff members and recruiting highly
motivated executives of proven ability,
company turnover increased by 35%
within two years.
Despite adverse market forces, the level of
activity has been maintained with
corresponding profitability. Recently
rewarded by the company with a Porsche.

September (year) – July (year)
Director of Purchasing and
Development responsible to the
Managing Director for researching
proposed development and
redevelopment projects, i.e. ensuring

cost-effectiveness, long-term viability, or quick resale profit potential; obtaining engineers' soil test reports; negotiating the purchase of greenfield sites and existing buildings, e.g. office-blocks, factories and warehouses; liaising with all relevant professions.

ACHIEVEMENT: Personally responsible for negotiating the purchase of a partially completed £800,000 development from the Moorland Bank. This development was subsequently completed and sold, with a net profit to the company of £240,000.

March (year) – September (year)
Buyer/Negotiator responsible for travelling throughout the UK, negotiating options on agricultural land, as well as purchasing land with outline planning permission. Required to liaise with architects and chief planning officers, and participate in the presentation of planning applications. Fought and won an appeal to the DOE over the refusal of planning permission to build a new office-block.
Four subordinate head office personnel.

Feb. (year) – Mar. (year) Midshire Estates Ltd
122–124 Clifton Road, Anytown, Midshire
– Estate Agents, Auctioneers and Valuers (30 branches)

Branch Manager (Midchester)
responsible to the Managing Director
for the efficient day-to-day running of
the branch, i.e. securing instructions to
sell house properties; preparing
valuations, newspaper advertisements
and property fact sheets; negotiating
sales; advising purchasers with regard to
mortgage facilities; liaising with clients'
solicitors.
Two subordinate negotiators, six full
and part-time administrative and clerical
staff.

Aug. (year)   Anytown Building Society
– Jan. (year)   188 New Road, Anytown, Midshire
– 400 branches

January (year) – January (year)
Assistant Manager (North End Branch).

August (year) – January (year)
Administrative Clerk/Cashier
(Midchester Branch).

19

Complete CVs

A JOINER

PERSONAL DETAILS

Full Name:	George Donkin
Address:	14 Westbourne Road, Anytown, Midshire, XX1 1YY
Telephone No:	Anytown (01888) 888888
Date of Birth:	28th February (year)
Place of Birth:	Anytown, Midshire
Nationality:	British
Marital Status:	Married with son aged 15 and daughter aged 12
Driving Licence:	Current (full)
Passport No:	X 88888Y – expires August (year)

CURRICULUM VITAE

EDUCATION AND QUALIFICATIONS

*Sept. (year)
– July (year)*   Anytown Comprehensive School
Anytown, Midshire

June (year) CSE
Woodwork   (1)

Art	(1)
Engineering Drawing	(2)
Mathematics	(3)
English	(3)
History	(4)

Sept. (year)
– June (year)

Anytown College of Further and Higher
Education
– Day Release and Evening Classes

June (year)
City and Guilds of London Institute
Craft Certificate – Carpentry and
Joinery

EXPERIENCE

Feb. (year)
– to date

F Lynch & Son Ltd
217 Beacon Road, Garth Industrial
Estate,
Anytown, Midshire
– Builders, Shopfitters and Bar Fitters

Foreman Joiner on a £5m club refit and
extension. Responsible for the
supervision of thirty-eight joiners,
plumbers, electricians, bricklayers and
labourers engaged in the construction of
period bars, static and revolving stages,
all backstage facilities and a restaurant.

Oct. (year)
– Feb. (year)

J S Rigg (Builders) Ltd
45 Aqueduct Street, Anytown, Midshire

Foreman Joiner – supervision of twenty
joiners on the rebuilding of a 300
bedroom, 4 star hotel, damaged by fire;
bars; studdings; spiral staircases;
hardwood dance floors; door casings.

Nov. (year)	H P Construction and Design Ltd
– Oct. (year)	106–108 Victoria Road, Anytown, Midshire
	– Public House and Hotel Refurbishment Contractors

Joiner in the workshop making bars, back-fittings, door casings and mock period timber beams.
Worked on site – fixing false ceilings and raised areas.

Mar. (year)	E F Wall & Sons Ltd
– Nov. (year)	81–83 Clay Street, Anytown, Midshire
	– Building Contractors

Joiner – first, second and final fix on new houses.

Nov. (year)	Oak Tree Joinery
– Mar.	28–30 Coronation Road, Anytown,
(year)	Midshire
	– Manufacturers of Replacement Doors and Windows

Bench Hand/Installer making and fitting uPVC windows and doors.

July (year)	Joseph Yorke & Co Ltd
– Nov. (year)	35 Oak Road, Anytown, Midshire
	– Building Contractors

July (year) – November (year)
Joiner – first, second and final fix on an exclusive housing development.

July (year) – *July (year)*
Apprentice Joiner (Indentured) – two
years in the joinery shop; two years
supervised on-the-job training.

OUTSIDE ACTIVITIES

Hobbies   Playing squash, family activities and
reading.

References   Available on request.

A RETAIL SALES MANAGER

PERSONAL DETAILS

Full Name: James Smith
Address: 8 Ashburton Close, Anytown,
Midshire, XX1 1YY
Telephone No: Anytown (01888) 888888
Date of Birth: 19th July (year)
Place of Birth: Anytown, Midshire
Nationality: British
Marital Status: Married – no children
Driving Licence: Current (clean)

CURRICULUM VITAE

EDUCATION AND QUALIFICATIONS

Sept. (year)   St George's High School
– July (year)   Anytown, Midshire

June (year) GCE 'O' Level
Mathematics   (A)
English Language   (B)
History   (B)
Geography   (B)

Physics	(C)
Chemistry	(C)
Biology	(C)
English Literature	(C)

June (year) GCE 'A' Level
| Mathematics | (B) |
| History | (D) |

TRAINING

Fashionwear Shops plc

Feb. (year)	Training the Trainer	(1 week)
Oct. (year)	Staff Appraisal	(2 days)
July (year)	Man Management/	
	Leadership	(2 days)
May (year)	Computerised Stock Control	(2 days)
Oct. (year)	Motivating the Customer	(1 day)

EXPERIENCE/ACHIEVEMENTS

Oct. (year)
– to date
Fashionwear Shops Plc
121–129 Arcadia Road, Anytown,
Midshire
– 372 branches nationwide

January (year) – to date
General Manager (Midchester)
responsible to the Area Manager for
meeting sales budgets and controlling
the expenditure budget to set
parameters.
Duties include development of sales
staff; conducting weekly staff meetings;
attending monthly management
meetings; cost control (including
cleaning and maintenance); presentation
and display; stock control; ensuring
compliance with health and safety at
work legislation.

ACHIEVEMENT: 12% increase in business turnover in first full financial year.

October (year) – January (year)
Assistant Manager (Northend) responsible for the training and motivation of sales staff (10) using EPOS; completing staff timesheets and appraisals; stock control; security of cash and premises (key holder); presentation and display.

Nov. (year)
– Oct. (year)
Kelly & Smart Ltd
71–75 Burlingham Road, Anytown, Midshire

–Ladies' and Gents' Fashions
(5 branches)

Manager (Anytown) responsible to the Financial Director for the day-to-day running of the business. Duties included recruitment and training of staff (5); designing window and interior displays; formulating and placing local advertisements; balancing daily takings; banking; submitting a weekly trading analysis; security (key holder).

ACHIEVEMENT: Consistently exceeded agreed budgets, despite a strong presence from three similar retail shops within a distance of five hundred metres.

July (year)
– Nov. (year)
Simm's Ltd
44–52 Henry Street, Anytown, Midshire
– Departmental Store (80 branches)

Floor Supervisor (Children's Wear) – security of stock and cash; daily balancing of tills; float provision; dealing with complaints; ensuring compliance with regulations.

July (year) *– July (year)*	King's Menswear 18–20 Underdown Road, Anytown, Midshire – (Established in 1868)

January (year) – July (year)
Sales Assistant.

July (year) – January (year)
Sales Trainee.

OUTSIDE ACTIVITIES

Hobbies   Swimming, snooker, cycling and watching football.

References   Available on request.

A NURSE

PERSONAL DETAILS

Full Name:	Brenda Ann Jones RGN
UKCC PIN No:	00Z0000X
Address:	84 Agnew Road, Anytown, Midshire, XX1 1YY
Telephone No:	Anytown (01888) 888888
Date of Birth:	21st July (year)
Place of Birth:	Anytown, Midshire
Nationality:	British
Marital Status:	Single
Driving Licence:	Current (clean)

CURRICULUM VITAE

EDUCATION AND QUALIFICATIONS

Sept. (year) *– July (year)*	Anytown High School Anytown, Midshire

June (year) GCE 'O' Level

Mathematics	(B)
English Language	(B)
English Literature	(B)
Geography	(C)
Physics	(C)
Biology	(C)

June (year) GCE 'A' Level

Mathematics with Statistics	(D)
Psychology	(E)

Sept. (year) *– Nov. (year)*	The Royal Albert Memorial Hospital School of Nursing

November (year) RGN qualified

TRAINING

Jan. (year)	Assessor's Course	(2 days)
Aug. (year)	First Line Management	(4 days)
Mar. (year)	Lifting and Handling	(1 day)
June (year)	Intensive Care	(1 week)
Nov. (year)	HIV/Drugs Misuse	(2 days)

Professional Association

Member of the Royal College of Nursing

EXPERIENCE

Feb. (year)
– to date

Anytown Royal Hospital
Redwing Road, Anytown, Midshire

September (year) – to date
Staff Nurse (Grade E) on night duty in
the Acute General Surgical Ward (38
beds).
Duties include dealing with massive
injury patients needing emergency
surgery; major abdominal surgical cases
and patients with peripheral vascular
disease. Supervising and teaching
student nurses; liaising with medical and
paramedical staff.

February (year) – September (year)
Staff Nurse (Grade D) on the Acute
Male Medical Ward (25 beds).
Many tracheostomy and ventilated
patients, and terminally ill patients with
cardiac problems. Empathised with
anxious and bereaved relatives.

Sept. (year)
– Feb. (year)

The Royal Albert Memorial Hospital
Anytown, Midshire

November (year) – February (year)
Staff Nurse (Grade D) on the Elderly
Persons' Rehabilitation Ward (23 beds).
Duties – medicine rounds; pressure sore
prevention; use of preventative
medicine; supervising rehabilitation
exercises; liaising with the
multi-disciplinary team.

September (year) – November (year)
Student Nurse – ward based learning
comprised a series of fourteen,
eight-week, placements, i.e.: Acute
General; Male Medical; Female
Medical; Male Surgical; Female
Surgical; Geriatric; Community;
Obstetric; Paediatric; Psychiatric; ENT;
Maternity; A & E; Orthopaedic.

OUTSIDE ACTIVITES

Hobbies   Walking, swimming and foreign travel.

References   Available on request.

A CHEF

PERSONAL DETAILS

Full Name:	Roland Geoffrey Tillotson
Address:	17 Abercrombie Road, Anytown, Midshire, XX1 1YY
Telephone No:	Anytown (01888) 888888
Date of Birth:	5th September (year)
Place of Birth:	Anytown, Midshire
Nationality:	British
Religion:	Christian
Marital Status:	Single
Next of Kin:	Mr & Mrs D G Tillotson (Parents) – address as above.
Driving Licence:	Current (clean)
Passport No:	X 888888Y – expires September (year)
Health:	Excellent

CURRICULUM VITAE

EDUCATION AND QUALIFICATIONS

Sept. (year)
– July (year)
The Oaks School
Anytown, Midshire

June (year) CSE
Mathematics   (2)
English   (2)
French   (2)
Geography   (3)
Engineering Drawing   (3)

Sept. (year)
– June (year)
Anytown College of Further and Higher
Education
– Full-time

*City and Guilds of London Institute
Certificates*
June (year) 706/1 (2 Passes)
June (year) 706/2 (1 Credit; 2 Passes)

Royal Society of Arts
June (year) Catering French (Pass)

*Royal Institute of Public Health and
Hygiene*
June (year) The Food Hygiene and
Handling Certificate

EXPERIENCE

Feb. (year)
– to date
The Kite Inn
Honeypot Lane, Anytown, Midshire
– Public House
– A la carte restaurant (85 covers); hot
bar meals

Chef preparing up to one hundred and thirty à la carte meals daily, plus one hundred to one hundred and twenty lunch-time and evening bar meals. Control of a second chef, a commis chef and two kitchen assistants; menu planning and costing (56% margin); purchasing stock; hygiene.

Sept. (year)
– Feb. (year)
Anytown Craft and Management Recruitment Ltd
93 Shipley Street, Anytown, Midshire
– Saudi Arabian Construction Site

Catering Manager responsible to the UK based General Manager for setting up and running a camp for fifteen hundred construction workers. Responsible for the provision of all meals; stock control; planning and costing; training and motivation of one hundred and twenty catering staff.

Mar. (year)
– Sept.
(year)
The Mile End Hotel
122–128 South Promenade, Anytown, Midshire
– 3 Star (65 en suite bedrooms)

Chef – provision of à la carte meals to the restaurant (120 covers); the dining-room (130 covers); two functions rooms. Provision of takeaway meals and bar snacks. Control of a second chef, four commis chefs and three kitchen assistants.

Apr. (year)
– Mar. (year)
Anytown Holiday Centre Ltd
Beach Road, Anytown, Midshire
– Holiday Camp

216

	Chef – control of seven cooks and five kitchen assistants, preparing two thousand plus fast-food meals daily.
Jan. (year) *– Apr. (year)*	University of Anytown Seafield Road, Anytown, Midshire
	Commis Chef (one of six) involved in the preparation of one thousand plus cafeteria meals daily, on a three week menu cycle.
Apr. (year) *– Jan. (year)*	The Bird Cage Restaurant Anytown, Midshire – Anglo-French Restaurant (65 covers)
	Commis Chef making croissants; soups; cakes and rolls; sorbets.
Aug. (year) *– Apr. (year)*	The Middle West Hotels Group Anytown, Midshire – 3 and 4 Star Hotels
	Commis Chef moving between the company's six hotels.
Aug. (year) *– Aug. (year)*	The Fiddler's Arms Green Lane, Anytown, Midshire – High-class Grill-Room Restaurant (60 covers)
	Trainee Chef.

OUTSIDE ACTIVITES

Hobbies	Sea fishing and cycling.
References	Available on request.

20

The Wrong Way To Write Your Own CV

– followed by a table of questions and answers.

Name: Michelle Brown   Address: 85 New Road,
Date of Birth: 28th March (year)   Anytown,
Marital Status: Single   Midshire,
Children: Darren – born 6th July (year)   XX1 1YY
Chantelle – born 2nd May (year)
Driving Licence: Yes

Education, Qualifications and Training

> Anytown High School (5 years)
> Anytown College of Further and Higher
> Education (2 years)
>
> Qualifications – 6 GCSE subjects
>   RSA Word Processing Certificate

Work Experience

> With having to take care of my children, I
> have not had a full-time job since leaving
> college. Darren is now at school, and my
> mum looks after him in the holidays.

Chantelle has started at nursery school and my boyfriend's mum takes her and picks her up, so I am now looking for a job.

I had a full-time job with Day, Knight & Co, Chartered Accountants, 8 Water Street, Anytown, and went to college in the evenings. But I had to leave Day, Knight & Co, to have Darren.
I started work as an Office Junior. Then they advertised for a Typist/Receptionist. I applied and I was given the position. I was more or less in charge of the office, until I left to have Darren.

Since Darren was born, I have worked three evenings a week as a Barmaid at the Dog and Partridge Inn, Ball Street, Anytown. I had two months off when Chantelle was born, but they took me on again because they said I was so good at the job.

During my last year at school, I was a Shelf Stocker at Anytown Supermarket. This helped me to develop an understanding of the work ethic and enabled me to enhance my interpersonal skills.

Hobbies and Interests
My hobbies are children, playing video games and socialising.

Question: *What is wrong with this CV?*

Answer: Just about everything. To begin with, the personal details appear to have been thrown at the paper, and then allowed to remain at the point of impact. The reader's eye will be darting from side to side across the page, in a frantic search for information. The need to offer a presentation which is easy for the eye to scan down is clearly illustrated here. Equally important is the selective use of underlining (or italics) which is non-existent in this example.

If the reader proves sufficiently determined to arrive at education, qualifications and training, he will find himself wondering about things like: GCSE subjects and grades of passes; day release or evening classes; starting and finishing dates.

It may be that the reader is the type who scans the career history first, in which case, the early sections will be of no interest to him, because the CV will go straight into the waste-bin.

Question: *Can you tell me which was her most recent job?*

Answer: Since Chantelle is the younger of her two children, and Chantelle's birth is given as the reason for her temporary absence from the Dog and Partridge, I would say that the second job was her most recent. But don't think about it too long, or you will soon be as muddle headed as she is.

Question: *She does seem a bit confused, doesn't she?*

Answer: The confusion is caused by her failure to think about what she was doing beforehand, in order to get a clear outline plan of what she was trying to convey. Instead, she has simply spilled the contents of her mind onto the paper, resulting in a composition which tells us at least as much about Darren and Chantelle, as it does about her work.

Even more off-putting is the obviously high opinion she has of herself, e.g. 'they took me on again because they said I was so good at the job'. When referring to her job change at Day, Knight & Co, she says, 'I applied and I was given the position'. These smug statements highlight the danger of using the first person singular (I). She goes on to compound her folly by saying 'I was more or less in charge of the office, until I left to have Darren'. Not only will vague statements of this kind fail to impress the reader, they will positively discourage him. Furthermore, in this instance he will have cause for serious doubts about the truth of what she is saying, because no self-respecting firm of chartered accountants would put someone like her in charge of the office.

Question: *What does she mean when she says of her job at the supermarket that 'This helped me to develop an understanding of the work ethic and enabled me to enhance my interpersonal skills'?*

Answer: I most emphatically believe that she does
not have the remotest idea what she
means. She must have read it somewhere
and thought it looked good.

What it means to me is that her career
has passed its peak, and that she should
resign herself to another forty years at
the Dog and Partridge.

Question: *Do you think that having two young
children will make it more difficult for her
to get a full-time job?*

Answer: Yes, especially so in this case where she
makes it very clear that because her
children are so important to her, they
should be of equal interest to the reader
of the CV. The truth is that his interest in
her children will not go beyond seeing
them as a possible obstacle to her
time-keeping and regular attendance at
work. She has unwittingly made sure
that this fear will occur to him.

There is no need to put children's
names in the CV either.

Question: *Do you think that socialising is a wise
thing to put down as an interest?*

Answer: In this case no. But we all know people
who genuinely like going around
meeting others. There is no harm in
saying this, provided there are two or
three other solid leisure pursuits to place
ahead of socialising.

Question: *Why do you consider it unwise for this
applicant to include socialising as an
interest?*

Answer: Because her only other interest, besides her children, is playing video games.

  If I were the person reading this CV and had bothered to read this far, I would guess that she probably spends an excessive amount of time on the other side of the bar at the Dog and Partridge. This is the wrong impression to give in a CV, since the reader might easily create an entirely false image of a bleary eyed, rolling drunkard, stumbling through the office door every morning two hours late.

Question: *Should she not have mentioned references?*

Answer: Yes, if she is able to provide them.

21

Problems, Problems

Question: *The way the career histories are presented in this book might be all right for most people, but what about someone like me? I am a Fitter/Welder with twenty-three years' experience, working on short-term contracts for so many companies that I lost count years ago.*

Answer: I do not claim that the career histories shown on the preceding pages are the only way of presenting your experience. But I do believe that they represent the best approach for someone writing their own CV, and probably doing it seriously for the first time. However, in this particular instance, I agree that using my chosen format would give rise to a long, over repetitive and tedious read, with negative results being a near certainty. So here we go with something tailored to this problem:

A FITTER/WELDER

Experience   *Large Bore Piling Contracts* – MMA, MIG and TIG.

Piling for tunnel retaining walls, wing and push walls; reinforcing cages; bridge supports; retaining walls for multi-storey hotels, flats and car parks; piling for sewers.

Manufacture – MMA, MIG and TIG to Lloyds standards.

Tanks, chutes and pressure vessels; steam, gas and petrochemical pipework, including carbon and stainless-steel overhead pipes; welding of angle and channel iron support brackets; small bore stainless-steel pipes (½"); stainless-steel ducting.

General

Welding coffer-dams.
Tacking and welding carbon steel.
Cutting out damaged hull sections on general cargo ships, using oxy-propane cutting equipment.
Using oxyacetylene in the repair of deck fittings.
Fitting out boiler houses and associated plant, to drawings and specifications and to Lloyds' standards.
Hospital installation of steam, gas and hot water systems.
Hospital installation of heating and ventilating systems; welding pipework in service ducts.

Fitting, welding and erecting sprinkler systems.
Installing heater batteries and thermostatic valves.
Installing chemical refrigeration plant.
Supervising teams of skilled tradesmen.
Liaising with all trades.

Principal Employers – last ten years to date

Bucholtz Foundations (UK) Ltd, Anytown
– Piling Contractors.

Bunn & Bateson Ltd, Anytown
– Heavy Engineering.

Bayland Piling (Anytown) Ltd.

Maxisenta Mechanical Services Ltd, Anytown.

L F Marsh (Anytown) Ltd
– Heating and Ventilation Contractors.

SGE Fabricators Ltd, Anytown.

Bray Bros Ltd, Anytown
– Civil Engineering.

Jupiter Engineering Ltd, Anytown.

Rutter Welding (Anytown) Ltd
– Structural Engineers.

Spark Engineering Ltd, Anytown.

Britt Site Services Ltd, Anytown
– Fabrication Contractors.

Although the career histories of skilled
tradesmen in the same field are never
exactly alike, the above mix will
resemble what could be expected in this
situation. By putting principal
employers as a sub-heading, we are in
effect saying, 'I can't remember them all,
but these are the main ones'.

In preparing the career history like
this, I would expect the completed CV to
be on three A4 pages, allowing for an
average take-up of space by the
education, qualifications and training. If
space was available, it would be
worthwhile inserting one or two
contracts immediately below each of the
employers listed, e.g.:

Bucholtz Foundations (UK) Ltd,
Anytown
– Piling Contractors.

M6 motorway bridge widening,
DSS multi-storey office-block.

Question: *Why not do all CVs this way?*

Answer: I much prefer to match the experience to
the employer or employers, with whom
the particular area of experience was
gained. The above example is a
compromise, made necessary in order to
get round a difficult situation.

Question: *My problem is that I have been pursuing two distinctly different careers. I have worked for some employers as a Chauffeur and for others as an Accounts Clerk. I was told to do a separate CV for each occupation, but then I was left with huge unexplained time gaps. If I put it all on one CV to avoid these gaps, it looks a bit ridiculous, so what can I do?*

Answer: This is what I call 'two for the price of one', meaning that when someone in this situation asks me to prepare their CV, I have no choice but to do two CVs for the price of one. Fortunately, it does not happen too often.

It is simply a matter of including both occupations in each CV, in a way which brings only one of them to the fore. In the first of the two examples below, the chauffeur is the prominent one, the accounts clerk being used only to fill the dreaded gaps. In the second example, the roles are reversed.

A CHAUFFEUR

EXPERIENCE

Oct. (year) – to date

Madewell Plastics (Anytown) Ltd
Hove Road, Garth Industrial Estate, Anytown, Midshire

Chauffeur to the Managing Director, Mr F P Glynn – driving a Rolls-Royce fifty thousand miles a year on business trips throughout England and Scotland. Much driving in Central London and

229

other major cities; extensive weekend and late night work; airport collection of business executives from overseas.

July (year) *– Oct. (year)*	Day, Knight & Co, Chartered Accountants 8 Water Street, Anytown, Midshire

Audit Clerk.

Apr. (year) *– July (year)*	Colonel A B Bowman-Smith The Birches, Forest Road, Anytown, Midshire – Lord Lieutenant of Midshire

Chauffeur driving a Rolls-Royce to official functions, and on holiday journeys to Switzerland and the South of France. Duties included driving shooting parties around the Colonel's country estate in a Range Rover, and helping the gamekeeper to recruit beaters.

Nov. (year) *– Apr. (year)*	Anytown Sports and Leisure Ltd 1–7 Victory Road, Anytown, Midshire

Accounts Clerk.

Jan. (year) *– Nov. (year)*	Mr Joe Yorke – London, Paris, Los Angeles – Stage and Screen Actor

Chauffeur in UK, France and the USA – driving Rolls-Royce, Ferrari, Mercedes-Benz, BMW and Porsche cars.

Aug. (year) *– Jan. (year)*	R & L Slack Ltd 68–70 Avenue Road, Anytown, Midshire – Plumbers' Merchants
	Accounts and Administration Clerk.
Mar. (year) *– Aug. (year)*	Maxisenta Motor Traction Co Ltd 25–33 Dunne Road, Anytown, Midshire – Luxury Coach Operators (45 coaches)
	Driver – UK and European holiday tours, e.g. France, Switzerland, Italy, Germany and Austria.
June (year) *– Mar.* *(year)*	H B Household Appliances Ltd 28–30 Shore Road, Anytown, Midshire
	Clerk/Cashier.

AN ACCOUNTS CLERK

EXPERIENCE

Oct. (year) *– to date*	Madewell Plastics (Anytown) Ltd Hove Road, Garth Industrial Estate, Anytown, Midshire
	Chauffeur to the Managing Director.
July (year) *– Oct. (year)*	Day, Knight & Co, Chartered Accountants 8 Water Street, Anytown, Midshire

Audit Clerk – preparing trading and profit and loss accounts for small traders and partnerships; keeping VAT records and preparing returns; calculating PAYE and national insurance.

Apr. (year) *– July (year)*	Colonel A B Bowman-Smith The Birches, Forest Road, Anytown, Midshire – Lord Lieutenant of Midshire

Chauffeur.

Nov. (year) *– Apr. (year)*	Anytown Sports and Leisure Ltd 1–7 Victory Road, Anytown, Midshire

Accounts Clerk – computer input of takings from squash and badminton courts, bowling alleys, games machines and vending machines.
Duties included liaison with all departments to correct errors; production of weekly cash sheets; banking.

Jan. (year) *– Nov. (year)*	Mr Joe Yorke – London, Paris, Los Angeles – Stage and Screen Actor

Chauffeur.

Aug. (year) *– Jan. (year)*	R & L Slack Ltd 68–70 Avenue Road, Anytown, Midshire – Plumbers' Merchants

Accounts and Administration Clerk –
computer input; preparing sales
invoices; verifying purchase invoices;
producing monthly sales and stock
sheets; dealing with telephone enquiries.

Mar. (year) *– Aug. (year)*	Maxisenta Motor Traction Co Ltd 25–33 Dunne Road, Anytown, Midshire – Luxury Coach Operators

Driver.

June (year) *– Mar. (year)*	H B Household Appliances Ltd 28–30 Shore Road, Anytown, Midshire

Clerk/Cashier – keeping sales and
purchase ledgers; typing materials orders;
computer input of stock data; checking
incoming delivery documentation;
reconciling cash with till rolls.

Question: *The career history examples do not
appear to offer much help to the
self-employed. Should they approach the
writing of their CVs in the same way as
everyone else?*

Answer: The self-employed generally fall into one
of two categories.

The first, and perhaps more common,
is tradesmen or salesmen working on an
hourly or commission basis. Apart from
reduced protection under the law, the
main difference between this type of
self-employment and employee status
lies in the method of payment. Duties
and responsibilities, time-keeping and
the standard of work requirements will
not necessarily differ to a large extent.

Therefore, the CV will be presented in the usual way.

The second category includes those who have been self-employed running their own business. While some prospective employers may be discouraged, by the possibility that these applicants might not conform easily to the disciplines of full-time employment, others will be aware that the customer is the most demanding master of all.

If long hours in excess of the accepted norm have been worked, week in and week out, this fact should be conveyed, as in the following career history:

Aug. (year) *– to date*	J Smith (Building Contractor) Lower Lane, Anytown, Midshire – New House Building; Extensions; Home Improvements etc. Proprietor – totally responsible for running the business with up to six skilled tradesmen and ten labourers. Working an average of sixty-five hours a week, responsibilities include purchasing materials; staff recruitment, motivation and control; preparation of tenders; book-keeping and VAT returns; liaising with all associated professions. Four contracts, each exceeding £200,000 in value, have been successfully completed during the last three years.

Question: *Would a prospective employer not wonder why the business was not continuing?*

234

Answer: Possibly. Therefore the applicant might make the following inclusion in an accompanying letter:

Although my business continues to make a satisfactory return, the long-term prospects are uncertain. For this reason, I have decided to seek full-time employment with a well established large company, strong enough to hold its own in this highly competitive field.

(Assuming of course, that this is the case, as it so often will be.)

For guidance on how the rest of the letter might read, attention should be paid to the chapter entitled, 'The Introductory Letter'.

Question: *What does the applicant put on his CV if he is currently out of work, following release from prison?*

Answer: I subscribe to the belief that he who is half clever enough to tell a lie will be clever enough to know better than to try it. Although it is known for applicants in this situation to make false statements, e.g. long-term unemployed, working for a friend, working overseas etc., the truth could emerge at an interview, or through a prospective employer making a thorough check on an individual's background.

Any applicant feeling inclined to attempt concealing a period of imprisonment should remember that it is a statutory offence to obtain employment by deception. Surely he would be better to be open about it and contend that his debt to society has been paid, and he intends to apply himself with great dedication, in order to regain the respect of his fellow beings?

Question: *Should those with disabilities disclose the fact on their CV?*

Answer: If an applicant is a registered disabled person, this should be entered in the personal details section.

Question: *I have been working continuously for the past fifteen years, but for most of the last seven I have been doing two jobs at once. How do I accommodate these in my CV?*

Answer: It is probable that, in this situation, the applicant will have been working as a full-time employee for one organisation and, in his spare time, as a part-time employee for one, or several other employers. Assuming the part-time experience to be relevant to the kind of work being sought, it should be dealt with immediately below the full-time career history, which will be set out in the usual way. After this, will appear:

Part-time Work Experience
– which will also run in reverse date order.

Unless the part-time work in question is of special importance, you should think hard before including it. The prospective employer might decide that if you continued with part-time work after joining him, your attention would be divided between the two jobs. This would certainly deter him, even if his fears were unjustified.

Question: *I am eighteen years old and have a full-time, unskilled job working in a slaughterhouse. Despite having obtained quite good GCSE grades, I see no chance of improving my career prospects.*

I have been advised to go back into full-time education and get some more qualifications, then my CV would look much more appealing. What do you think?

Answer: Go back into education and study for two good 'A' Level grades in solid subjects. These will command widespread respect from prospective employers reading your CV. Be wary of the marketing skills of institutions selling and running a range of alternative courses, some of which are looked upon with suspicion by employers.

Question: *I am forty and, although I have extensive experience in my work, I have little in the way of formal qualifications. I find this very discouraging when trying to write my CV. What should I do?*

Answer: Take heart. One of the best CVs I have ever written was for an engineer, whose only qualifications were his indentures. Some twenty years previously he had served a five year apprenticeship with an old established company, running its own, carefully devised in-house apprentice training scheme. This man, whose achievements were awesome, represented an outstanding example of qualification by experience.

Provided your CV lands on the right desk, all the reader will want to know is what you have done in your work. This will enable him to decide what you can do for him.

If your CV lands on the wrong desk, it will be read by a 'personnel professional', who might have little understanding of what he is reading. In the absence of a decorative array of certificates and diplomas, he will toss it aside with contempt.

You could also come to grief at the hands of a recruitment consultant who, until a fortnight earlier, might have been selling baked beans.

Obviously, your chances will be much better where someone with experience in your trade is involved in the recruitment process. This is more likely where a company is doing its own recruiting.

Question: *A colleague says that when a friend of his was writing his CV, he prefaced the career history with a brief statement, i.e.: 'A self-motivated and successful Sales Professional, able to apply his superbly developed interpersonal skills to attain maximum levels of profitable business growth, in the highly charged and challenging environment of a dynamic industrial commercial, import/export organisation'.*

What would you say to that?

Answer:　　　　I would say that this man is an
unprincipled line shooter, who should go
into politics at national level where he
will have a bright future.

　　The question highlights the growing
tendency by people and organisations in
all walks of life, to speak and write in
pretentious jargon instead of making
clear, simple statements.

　　This is the gloss culture, which has
spread out from its origins in the world
of advertising, to infiltrate the whole of
the public services sector and large areas
of industry and commerce, with
devastating consequences. If you allow
the gloss culture to creep into your CV,
you are in grave danger of being
identified with its two main objectives,
i.e. the concealment of poor standards
and the glorification of mediocrity.

Question:　　*I have prepared what I believe to be a*
perfectly good CV, but the job I am
applying for requires me to complete an
application form. Should I attach a copy
of my CV to the application form and
write on it – See enclosed CV?

Answer:　　　　No. Whilst a properly prepared CV can
be expected to provide two-thirds to
three-quarters of the information
required on most application forms,
there will still be questions, often very
important ones, which must be
answered. I suggest the following way of
dealing with this common problem: all
questions relating to personal details,
education, qualifications and training
should be answered in the usual way,

although it will often mean writing down again details which are already in the CV. Then read through the form carefully and answer any questions which are not catered for by the CV.

Where the career history or employment experience is concerned, the form may have only a relatively small area in which to insert the briefest of details, in which case, that is what must be done. However, when the form concludes with one, two or even more blank pages for details of previous employment, it is common practice to write – See enclosed CV – and attach a copy.

Consider also the problem of the large organisation which might distribute hundreds of returned application forms between several senior executives, with instructions to compile a list for first interview. Suppose that, say, question 10 is the important one. Visualise the difficulty if applicants have answered it by advising scrutiny of an attached CV. For this reason, some applicants frequently complete the application form in its entirety, particularly when the post on offer happens to be in the state sector.

It comes down in the end to an accurate assessment of each individual situation, e.g. size of company, type of business, kind of work being applied for.

Question: *I am in senior management and I am applying for a similar position, with better long-term prospects. I have been told that I should place a copy of my CV in a presentation folder, then send it in a matching sized envelope. But others say that this is going too far and if I do it the CV will be discarded with contempt because they will think I am a big-head. What should I do?*

Answer: For applicants in senior management, or in sales and marketing, presentation is of considerable importance. As in all things, views differ about what constitutes a pleasing presentation. Among the many job applicants I meet, it has become the norm for those who need to present themselves in this way to use an A4 'see through' perspex folder with a slim plastic spine clip. To complete the process, the CV should have a face (or front) page. In the centre of the face page should be typed:

CURRICULUM VITAE
OF
FORENAME(S) SURNAME

When the CV has been inserted securely in the folder, the introductory letter (see Chapter 22) should be clipped to the outside, and the whole package placed in an A4 envelope.

Question: *After my employer closed down, I was unemployed for over a year. I have now undergone retraining as an audio typist. How do I explain this interlude on my CV?*

Answer: Assuming the course took up a reasonable slice of the period of unemployment, the entry on your CV might read thus:

Nov. (year) Took advantage of this period of
– Oct. (year) unemployment to retrain, with a view to acquiring greater versatility.

(Details of this course will already have been inserted under education, qualifications and training.)

Question: *But I am confessing to a long period of unemployment. Surely that will ruin my prospects?*

Answer: You have shown that you are sufficiently self-motivated to have improved your range of skills, in order to get off the dole. If you conceal this period of unemployment by telling lies, you are in fact confessing in writing to an offence you have not committed, i.e. working whilst drawing unemployment benefit.

Question: *How long should a CV be?*

Answer: This brings us back into the territory of the baked bean selling recruitment consultant, the personnel professional and everyone else involved in human resource management (a typical example of gloss culturespeak). These, and other 'experts', will invariably tell you that on no account must your CV exceed two A4 pages. Their advice will be damaging in many cases.

The majority of CVs that I have prepared are on three A4 pages. Most of the remainder are on two or four pages, with a very small number exceeding four pages. In common with seasoned campaigners who have lived and worked in places across the world, I do not like to see a CV exceed three pages. Unfortunately, this cannot be taken as a hard and fast rule.

Consider the typical example of an applicant who is already in management, and is applying for a better paid job with even more responsibility than at present. He needs to give a comprehensive account of his experience and could well find that keeping down to three pages will do more harm than going onto a fourth.

Faced with a CV on, say, three and a half A4 pages, I have debated the question, 'Do we cut it down, or do we leave it?', with many job applicants, and the answer is not always the same. But there has to be a convincing reason for allowing the CV to encroach onto a fourth page. Applicants in this situation should do their utmost to keep down to three pages, but not by attempting to cram too much information onto each sheet. This leaves the reader hunting around in search of important material and he will lose patience. Do not try to 'cheat', by using small type and narrow margins. This will only make a quick initial scan difficult or, where the reader is 'visually challenged', downright impossible.

Consider also the young student or graduate, whose CV should not really exceed two A4 pages. A large amount of part-time work for numerous employers, coupled with an extensive academic record and the names and addresses of two referees, makes a two page presentation an unrealistic goal. Here again you have to do your best, but be careful not to undersell yourself.

Question: *Should I send a photograph with my CV?*

Answer: Usually an applicant will only enclose a photograph when requested to do so, e.g. when applying for any position where appearance is all important.

Question: *But I am an attractive twenty-two year old female, applying for a job as a dental nurse. Although the advertisement does not ask for a photograph, surely it could make all the difference, could it not?*

Answer: Indeed it could, especially if the dentist's wife is helping him to vet the applications. In that case, being of middle age and blessed with great ugliness could be virtues of a high order.

22

The Introductory Letter

When replying to an advertisement for a job vacancy, the CV must always be accompanied by an introductory letter.

The quality of the letter is at least as important as the quality of the CV, in some cases more so. Applicants who are equipped with a good CV might fail repeatedly to secure an invitation to attend an interview because of a bad letter.

Remember that the letter is the opening shot. It creates the first impression which is the one by which most people judge. An impressive letter can overcome the odd weakness in a CV. Conversely, a poor letter might cause a perfectly good CV to be thrown in the waste-bin.

The letter must be short, crisp and clear, opening with the name and date of issue of the publication in which the advertisement appeared. If a reference number is given, it should be displayed in the top left-hand corner of the letter and likewise, on the envelope.

In the second paragraph, the applicant should say briefly why he believes that he is a suitable candidate for the job.

The third paragraph should contain a good reason why that job is particularly desirable.

The concluding part of the letter should supply routine

information, e.g. current rate of pay if the advertisement requests this; period of notice required by present employer, and the length of notice needed to attend an interview.

The letter should reflect the kind of person from whom the recruiter is hoping to hear. This requirement is clearly illustrated in the three specimen letters below:

From a plumber

5 Avenue Road,
Anytown,
Midshire,
XX1 1YY

Mr P A Scott-Brown,   Date
Adapt Mechanical Services Ltd,
118–120 Hunts Road,
Anytown,
Midshire,
XX1 1YY

Dear Sir,

I have seen your advertisement, in the Construction Gazette of July 8th, for plumbers to work on a Dutch chemical factory contract.

My experience includes work of a similar kind, e.g. the Cann Chemical Factory in Nigeria, for Hull & Blackwell Ltd.

Having just completed a hospital building contract in Saudi Arabia as a Foreman Plumber with Bates, Barlow (Construction) Ltd, I am now looking for the kind of work offered by your advertisement.

A copy of my CV is enclosed and, if you decide to see me for an interview, I could attend at short notice.

Yours faithfully,

Martin Smith

Let us change now from the purely practical style of the tradesman to what might be expected of the high-powered, young executive burning with ambition.

Your Ref: XX 111

> 5 The Close,
> Anytown,
> Midshire,
> XX1 1YY

Mr P R Whiteside,   Date
Personnel Manager,
Wayside Box & Packaging Co Ltd,
6–10 Wayside,
Anytown,
Midshire,
XX1 1YY

Dear Sir,

Your advertisement in the Daily Post of May 12th for a Regional Sales Manager to increase the rate of business growth in the Southern Counties is of great interest to me.

You will see from the enclosed CV that I have had extensive experience in negotiating at all levels, including much successful sharp end contact.

Whilst relations with my employers remain very good, the job does not hold the same prospect of advancement that would exist in a larger organisation.

My employers would require one month's notice of leaving. I would appreciate the opportunity of an interview, and it would help if I could have three working days' notice of the date.

Yours faithfully,

James Smith

Changing the style yet again, we see what someone applying for a clerical job might write.

29 Brook Avenue
Anytown,
Midshire,
XX1 1YY

Reville, Walker & Bates   Date
Chartered Architects,
173 Avondale Road,
Anytown,
Midshire,
XX1 1YY

Dear Sirs,

I would like to be considered for the position of Secretary/Typist, advertised in the Daily Gazette of April 8th.

A copy of my CV is enclosed, and you will see that in addition to my RSA Word Processing Certificate, I do have the required GCSE grades in English and Mathematics. I also have three years' experience as a secretary/typist.

Having moved into the area only recently, I am looking for permanent employment in secretarial work, where the duties and responsibilities would be similar to those in my last job (salary £xx,xxx).

The opportunity of an interview would be much appreciated, and I could attend at short notice.

Yours faithfully,

Julie Brown

Although these three specimen letters display clearly the necessary differences in style, they should only be viewed as a loose guide since, in order to draft an introductory job application letter accurately, you need the advertisement before you.

23

The Speculative Approach

Many job seekers pass the time between applying for advertised vacancies by 'blitzing' companies in a particular field of activity. An advantage of using this ploy is that once drafted, the same letter can be used repeatedly. The disadvantage is that the process amounts to a series of long shots in the dark, and some employers have become ill-disposed to such treatment.

However, if this course of action is to be taken, it must be done properly. The first step is to decide which organisations to approach. Compile an initial list of (say) ten companies. Discover the names and job titles of the company officials to whom the letter is to be addressed.

I emphasise the importance of identifying the individual personnel manager, recruiting officer, head of department, etc. If this is not done, or done wrong, the application may not find its way to the right person. Even if it does, he will not give it as much weight as he would when seeing his name on the envelope, as well as on the letter.

A brief telephone call to each of the companies selected is usually all that is necessary, since the switchboard operator is likely to be able to supply the name and job title of the official concerned. Items for special attention are his initials, and the correct spelling of his name.

Having set the stage, next comes the composition of the letter which need be little more than a courteous introduction, with a view to being placed on file.

6 The Avenue
Anytown,
Midshire,
XX1 1YY

Mr J A Smith,   Date
Personnel Manager,
Wayside Chemical Products Ltd,
18–22 Wayside,
Anytown,
Midshire,
XX1 1YY

Dear Sir,

Although you may not have any vacancies advertised at the moment, I am writing to ask if you might be able to offer me a position as a chemical research analyst.

The enclosed CV will show that, in addition to possessing the necessary qualifications, I have gained a broad range of experience, which I am sure could be used to advantage in working for your company.

My employers require one month's notice of leaving. I would appreciate the opportunity of an interview if a vacancy occurs, and five working days' notice would be helpful.

Yours faithfully

Peter Bailey

When the job application, or speculative approach, letter has been composed, one question still remains: should it be typed or handwritten?

When replying to an advertised vacancy, this question will sometimes already have been answered, e.g. where applicants are required to apply in their own handwriting. The usual response, in this case, is to enclose a handwritten letter with a copy of the CV, although some applicants go the whole hog, and hand copy their CV as well. The merits of such eagerness to please are at best debatable, except where the advertisement specifies a handwritten CV.

Applicants who have reached senior management level will often dismiss any suggestion of handwritten correspondence, preferring to offer a business-like presentation.

Sometimes a male applicant will ask his partner to write the letter, or complete the job application form as the partner's handwriting is neater than the applicant's. No doubt this practice has caused the odd furrowed brow in the world of graphology!

HOW NOT TO WRITE A JOB APPLICATION LETTER

6 Firtree Grove,
Anytown,
Midshire,
XX1 1YY

The Manager,   Date
Anytown Saw-Mills Ltd,
Anytown Industrial Estate,
Anytown,
Midshire,
XX1 1YY

Dear Sir,

I believe you are looking for an office manager, and I think I could be the man for the job.

The enclosed CV will show you what I am capable of. From it, you will see that I have had wide experience in managing offices in many different industries, and I believe this is the only way to learn.

Living as I do very close to your premises, I would

251

appear to be ideally located, and I should be pleased to attend an interview if you should very kindly invite me to one.

Yours faithfully,

Jim Brown

The opening of this letter is too casual. If the applicant has heard that there is a job vacancy with the company, he should locate the advertisement and apply in the normal way. If, on the other hand, he has heard secretly from a friend that there might be a position open but no advertisement has yet been placed, he should try a speculative approach.

The applicant continues in a high-handed manner, telling the reader to see 'what I am capable of' and then goes on to say, 'I believe this is the only way to learn'. Who does he think he is? This statement clearly implies that the reader would be wrong to disagree.

In emphasising that his home is near to their place of business, the applicant obviously believes this will strengthen the case. The opposite could be just as easily implied. He has made it clear that his main reason for applying is that it would be a convenient place for him to go to work.

Finally, after sailing through nearly the whole of the letter in this haughty manner, the applicant suddenly turns to the other extreme. He starts to crawl, by saying with regard to an interview, 'if you should very kindly invite me to one'. The reader will be left with an easy decision, and this sickening letter will rightly end up in the waste-bin.

And Finally

Although this book is bound to help some more than others, it is hard to see how anyone in the job market who has read it completely can have failed to learn something of value.

While many job applicants ruin their prospects by trying too hard and appearing boastful, a similar number wreck their chances by selling themselves short. This is the modesty factor. It prevents the applicant from giving a good account of himself, but may go deeper, and cause him even to be unaware of the many useful qualities he possesses.

Just one of the aims in writing this book has been to try and show the reader how to make the good first impression, which is so vitally important. Even if the job being sought does not exactly match an applicant's career background, a good presentation might cause the recruiter to say, 'He isn't exactly what we have in mind, but he certainly seems like a chap worth meeting. I think we'll have him in for a chat'.

In the end, it comes down to being as sure as you can be, that your CV is a concise, factual and attractive document.

Index